DISCARDED

DAVID HUME

A. H. Basson

GREENWOOD PRESS, PUBLISHERS
WESTPORT, CONNECTICUT

Library of Congress Cataloging in Publication Data

Cavendish, Anthony Pike, 1916–
   David Hume.

   Reprint of the ed. published by Penguin Books,
Harmondsworth, Middlesex, in series: Pelican philosophy
series and no. A428 of Pelican books.
   Includes bibliographical references and index.
    1. Hume, David, 1711–1776.
B1498.C3 1981   192   78–26704
ISBN 0–313–20668–6

Copyright © A. H. Basson, 1958

First published 1958

Reprinted with the permission of Penguin Books Ltd.

Reprinted in 1981 by Greenwood Press
A division of Congressional Information Service, Inc.
88 Post Road West, Westport, Connecticut 06881

Printed in the United States of America

10 9 8 7 6 5 4 3 2 1

CONTENTS

EDITORIAL FOREWORD

THE series to which this book belongs is devoted to the history and to the problems of philosophy in all its various branches. It is designed both to interest the specialist and to attract the general reader. Beyond this, the contributors to it have been left free to handle their chosen subject in their own way: they have not been selected with a view to advancing the opinions of any one philosophical school.

In his own time, David Hume was esteemed more highly as an historian and an essayist than as a philosopher. In the nineteenth century he was celebrated chiefly for his scepticism; his main achievement was thought to be that of having been the means of awakening Kant from his 'dogmatic slumber'. It is only in recent years that he has obtained his due acknowledgement as a very great philosopher in his own right. As Mr Basson shows, his contributions both to the theory of knowledge and to ethics are highly original and important. Hume is also a master of English prose; almost too much so for a philosopher. The ease and lucidity of his style tend to mask the profundity of his thought. It is astonishing to find how much of what is thought to be distinctive in modern analytical philosophy was already foreshadowed in Hume's work.

A. J. AYER

CHAPTER I

HUME'S LIFE
AND PHILOSOPHICAL WORKS

I

DAVID HUME was born at Edinburgh on the 26 April 1711 (Old Style).[1] He was the second son of Joseph Hume, or Home, proprietor of the estate of Ninewells, in Berwickshire. His mother was a daughter of Sir David Falconer of Newton. Joseph Hume died in 1713, and his widow did not remarry, but devoted herself thereafter entirely to the rearing and education of her children. She appears to have been a woman of strong character and considerable intelligence, commanding the respect and affection of her family. The Humes of Ninewells were gentry of the middle sort, and had extensive connexions with other families of the Scottish Border.

Nothing is known of Hume's early childhood, and he does not seem to have exhibited any remarkable precocity. In 1723 he entered at the University of Edinburgh, where he remained probably for three or four years, and where he attended William Scot's class in Greek. No doubt he attended other lectures as well, and these may have included Colin Drummond's 'Rational and Instrumental Philosophy', and William Law's 'Pneumatical and Ethical Philosophy'. Drummond is known to have been interested in the New Philosophy, associated with the names of Newton and Locke. Law's 'Pneumatical Philosophy', that is, mental philosophy, appears to have included 'metaphysical inquiry into subtle substances imperceptible to the senses, and known only through their operations; proof of the immortality of the soul; Natural Theology, or the demonstration of the existence and the attributes of God'. All these things are treated of in Hume's own works, albeit in a negative and destructive manner. One extant manuscript, entitled 'An Historical Essay on Chivalry and Modern Honour', is said to date from

9

his student days. It exhibits the subtlety and acuteness, and also some of the preoccupations to be found in his later work. Hume himself says that the *Treatise of Human Nature* was 'projected before he left College', but this is scarcely credible except perhaps in the most tenuous sense. He left Edinburgh University before he was sixteen.

After leaving the University, Hume made some attempt to prepare himself for the profession of advocate, but he did not find legal studies to his taste, and soon abandoned the notion. He seems already to have been absorbed in philosophical speculations. In the autumn of 1729 he was seized with a kind of nervous breakdown, the effects of which persisted intermittently for the next five years. The nature and causes of this crisis are, of course, unknown. Hume himself wrote a long memoir on the subject, in the form of a letter to an unknown physician, but, as might be expected, this memoir is tantalizingly vague at many points. He was at this time interested in the Stoic system of morality, as represented by Seneca and Plutarch, and he practised the regimen of that school, perhaps with too much enthusiasm. In later life his ethical views were sharply opposed to those of the Stoics. Hume's illness was not accompanied by serious depression or anxiety, he mentions 'a weakness rather than a lowness of spirits' and 'a coldness and desertion of the spirit', such as has been reported by mystics and other such fanatical people. These symptoms interrupted and prevented his philosophical speculations, but did not unfit him for any other activity. In 1734 he decided to abandon philosophy for a while.

Hume's attempt to leave philosophy was short-lived, and in the summer of 1734 he retired to France, where he remained for three years, and succeeded in completing the *Treatise of Human Nature*. During this period he managed, by the exercise of great frugality, to subsist on a very small paternal inheritance. The desire for independence was an important factor in Hume's life, and it is worth noting that his capacity for work returned to him as soon as he left home. He returned to London in 1737. The first two volumes of the

Treatise were published in 1739, and the third volume in the following year.

Hume expected immediate recognition for his masterpiece, and the cool reception accorded to it was a severe disappointment to him. Reviews appeared in several learned journals in England, France, and Germany, but they were either condescending or sarcastic or both. They show no real understanding of the work, although it was regarded by some as showing promise for the future. No doubt the reviewers were influenced by irrelevancies, such as Hume's obvious contempt for religious dogma, and scepticism is always shocking and incomprehensible to those who have no natural inclination towards it. On the other hand, no one who has read and tried to understand the *Treatise* can altogether blame those who were first required to assess it.

In 1741 and 1742 Hume brought out two volumes entitled *Essays Moral and Political*. Much of their contents was of a slight, even frivolous character, and they enjoyed more immediate success than the *Treatise*. In 1744, at the age of thirty-three, Hume applied for the vacant chair in philosophy at Edinburgh, but he was rejected on religious grounds. The contempt for religious dogma which pervades everything he wrote was an embarrassment to him throughout his life. In January of 1745 he received an invitation to become tutor to the Marquis of Annandale, which he accepted.

Of Hume's residence with the Marquis perhaps the less said the better. The Marquis was in fact insane, and 'keeper' would be a more apt title than 'tutor' for Hume's position in the household. His situation was complicated, and ultimately rendered untenable by the presence of a certain Captain Vincent, who held a commission from the Marquis to conduct some of his business. There seems little doubt that Vincent was an unpleasant and evil character, although the exact nature and extent of his wickedness cannot now be ascertained. Hume certainly formed the opinion that Vincent was a chief agent in intrigues concerning the inheritance of some of the Annandale property, and he involved himself, unnecessarily perhaps, in what was going on. But the letters we have, vague as they are, give the impression that Vincent was not merely engaged in an attempt to secure part of his employer's property for himself, but had other plans and intentions of an even more sinister colour. The outcome of Hume's opposition to these schemes was his ignominious dismissal in 1746. Vincent himself died a few months later, and so his aims remain unknown and unfulfilled.

Immediately upon his removal from this dark scene, Hume was offered the post of secretary to General St Clair. This gentleman had been commissioned to lead a military expedition, which was at first intended against the French settlements in Canada, but which ended in an unsuccessful raid on the coast of Brittany. The failure was due, not so much to the incompetence of its leaders, as to the ignorance and vacillation of politicians. Hume obviously enjoyed the affair, and performed his duties with success, being ultimately promoted to the position of judge-advocate. He returned to England in March 1747.

After a few months with his brother at Ninewells, Hume was again invited by General St Clair to attend him as secretary, this time on a secret military embassy to Vienna and Turin. The object of the embassy was to secure more active support from our allies in the War of the Austrian Succession, but its efforts were made unnecessary by the treaty of Aix-la-Chapelle. Hume had plenty of time and opportunity for social activities, in which he engaged himself with enthusiasm. His peculiar childlike innocence of mind, combined with a complete absence of jealousy and rancour, and a certain solidity of temperament, made him popular, especially among women, a fact which he not infrequently records with mild complacency. Hume's physical appearance at this time is also recorded for us by Lord Charlemont:

Nature, I believe, never formed any man more unlike his real character than David Hume. The powers of physiognomy were baffled by his countenance; neither could the most skilful in that science, pretend to discover the smallest trace of the faculties of his mind, in the unmeaning features of his visage. His face was broad and fat, his mouth wide, and without any other expression than that of imbecility. His eyes vacant and spiritless and the corpulence of his whole person, was far better fitted to communicate the idea of a turtle-eating alderman, than of a refined philosopher. His speech in English was rendered ridiculous by the broadest Scotch accent, and his French was, if possible, still more laughable; so that wisdom never before disguised herself in so uncouth a garb.

Hume's simplicity, his accent, and his rustic appearance, often made him the victim of witticisms and practical jokes, not always of the most kindly nature, but which he never failed to take in good part. While in Italy he suffered a severe attack of fever.

The most important material result of all these employments for Hume was the attainment of financial independence. In 1748 he was, so he tells us, 'now Master of near a thousand Pound', and for the next fifteen years he devoted himself entirely to literary work, residing first at Ninewells, and then, after the marriage of his brother in 1751, with his sister in Edinburgh. The *Philosophical Essays* (afterwards called the *Enquiry*) *concerning the Human Understanding*, and *Three Essays Moral and Political*, appeared in 1748. The *Enquiry concerning the Principles of Morals* appeared in 1751, *Political Discourses* in 1752, and *Four Dissertations* in 1757. The first draft of the *Dialogues concerning Natural Religion* dates from 1750, but these were not published until 1779, after Hume's death. The six volumes of his *History of England* came out between 1754 and 1762, so completing his literary labours. He applied unsuccessfully for the chair of logic at Glasgow University in 1752, and in the same year he was elected Keeper of the Advocates Library in Edinburgh, resigning this office in 1757.

In 1763 Hume accepted an invitation from the Marquis of Hertford, the newly appointed ambassador to the court of France, to attend him as a personal secretary with the further prospect of an official appointment as secretary to the embassy. By this time he was securely possessed of the literary fame which he had always sought, and which rested then on his historical, rather than on his purely philosophical works.

13

But great though his reputation was in England and Scotland, it was a small thing compared with the esteem in which he was held in France. His arrival in Paris seems to have been a literary and social event of the first magnitude. No doubt the respect felt for his writings was genuine and entirely justified, but it is a little more difficult to account for his extraordinary personal popularity in France. It was something more than a passing fashion, as is attested by the puzzled and envious letters of his contemporaries. These usually contain a sort of standard comment which may be represented as follows: 'David Hume is clumsy, oafish in appearance, he is heavy and lacking in grace, he speaks French very badly, and with an intolerable Scottish accent, and yet all the most beautiful women compete for his company and no social function is complete without him, I cannot understand it.' One concludes that there must have been some aspect of his character which is not fully communicated to us, either in his own writings, or in the reports of his contemporaries.

Hume did not receive his official appointment as secretary to the embassy until the summer of 1765. A few days later Lord Hertford was recalled, and Hume remained as chargé d'affaires in Paris until the following November, when the new ambassador, the Duke of Richmond, presented his credentials. Hume appears to have performed the duties attaching to his official position with tact and efficiency: he scarcely had any opportunity for feats of diplomatic brilliance. He returned to England early in 1766. In 1767 he was appointed an Under-Secretary of State, a position from which he resigned in 1769. The remainder of his life was spent in retirement, and was not interrupted by any remarkable events. He died after a rather long and tedious illness in 1776.

II

The edition of Hume's philosophical works used for this study is that of T. H. Green and T. H. Grose,[2] in four volumes, published by Longmans, Green, & Co., in 1875. The system of reference is prefaced to the Notes at the end of this book. In general, numeration of the *Essays*, and page references apply to the Green and Grose edition. References by book, chapter, section, and paragraph apply to any edition of Hume's works.

The topics treated of by Hume divide naturally under five heads: Epistemology, Psychology, Morals, Politics and Economics, and Religion. The sources for Hume's opinions on these topics are accordingly classified as follows.

EPISTEMOLOGY: *Treatise*, Book I (1739), *An Enquiry concerning Human Understanding* (1748).

PSYCHOLOGY: *Treatise*, Book II (1740), *A Dissertation on the Passions* (1757).

MORALS: *Treatise*, Book III (1740), *An Enquiry concerning the Principles of Morals* (1751), *A Dialogue* (1751).

POLITICS AND ECONOMICS: *Treatise*, Book III (Part 2), *Essays*, Part I (1741), numbers 2–9 and 12; *Essays*, Part 2 (1752).

RELIGION: *Essays*, Part I, number 10; *An Enquiry concerning Human Understanding*, Sections 10 and 11; *The Natural History of Religion* (1757); *Dialogues concerning Natural Religion* (1779); *Of the Immortality of the Soul* (1777).

Hume's psychology, that is to say, his theory of the passions, will not be discussed in this book, except incidentally in so far as it bears directly on more strictly philosophical matters. His politics and economics must also pass unnoticed. This leaves us with the epistemology, morals, and religion. Some preliminary observations of a general character must now be made on Hume's treatment of each of these three topics.

EPISTEMOLOGY: The chief difficulty for the expositor consists in relating the contents of the *Treatise*, Book I, to the *Enquiry concerning Human Understanding*. A problem exists because Hume disowned the *Treatise*, and recommended the *Enquiry* as the only satisfactory expression of his opinions. It would be reasonable to follow this recommendation if the *Enquiry* were a substantial advance on the *Treatise;* if, for example, difficulties which are left unsolved in the *Treatise* were solved, or even discussed more fully in the *Enquiry*. But this is not the case. The *Enquiry* is certainly a clearer and more readily intelligible work than the *Treatise*, but these desirable features are secured, not by solving difficulties, but by ignoring them. A brief comparison of contents will indicate the relation obtaining between the two books.

The *Treatise*, Book I, really discusses two distinct topics. These are, first, the nature and extent of human knowledge, and second, the nature of certain entities, namely, space, time, causality, the physical world, and the mind. The latter discussions are really ontology rather than epistemology, and it is in the field of ontology that most of Hume's difficulties arise. Generally speaking, the *Enquiry concerning Human Understanding* follows the plan of the *Treatise*, but omitting all ontological discussions, except for causality, which is treated in a simplified manner. It is possible that Hume felt these omissions to be justified because, for reasons which may be conjectured, he was chiefly interested in establishing a sceptical theory of knowledge, rather than in ascertaining the nature of these other entities or concepts. That this is likely may be seen from the fact that, although he admits the difficulties in his account of the mind, and himself observes that they seem to be insuperable, he does not for one moment entertain the notion that this might cast doubt upon the validity of his general theory. If ontology cannot be made to fit his theory of knowledge, so much the worse for ontology.

The omission of Hume's theories of space and time is perhaps no great loss, but his theories of the physical world and of the mind cannot be neglected. For all their faults they form an important contribution to philosophy. Furthermore, the epistemological discussions in the *Treatise* contain many subtleties which are passed over in the *Enquiry*. Consequently the plan adopted in this exposition is to follow the *Treatise*, Book I, with the omission of the part on space and time.

MORALS: The problem with respect to Hume's moral philosophy is superficially similar to the problem of his epistemology and ontology. We have two versions, the *Treatise*, Book III, and the *Enquiry concerning the Principles of Morals;* he disowns the former and recommends the latter. Here, however, it is not simply a matter of omissions. Mr Selby-Bigge goes so far as to say that there is 'a very remarkable change of tone, or temper, which, even more than particular statements, leads him to suppose that the system of Morals in the *Enquiry* is really and essentially different from that in the *Treatise*.'[3] The present writer cannot claim to have solved this problem satisfactorily, and will state his position without attempting to justify it. It is assumed, then, that the only parts of Hume's moral philosophy that are of real importance are (*i*) his theory that moral judgements are a matter of feeling and not of rational conviction, and (*ii*) his belief that the doctrine of free will is irrelevant to morals. Hume's discussion of the particular virtues and vices is psychologically interesting, but not philosophically important. In the present exposition the arguments of the *Treatise* are considered and examined.

A second point arises in connexion with Hume's moral philosophy. Professor Kemp Smith has argued very convincingly that Hume's first interest was in morals rather than in epistemology.[4] His opinion is supported by early letters and memoranda. The fact is of prime importance for the student of the development of Hume's thought, and in fixing the exact function and purpose of his philosophical enquiries. Nevertheless, from the purely philosophical point of view, epistemology naturally takes first place, and is the part of Hume's work upon which his fame as a philosopher chiefly rests. I have therefore followed the natural order of exposition, which Hume himself adopted.

RELIGION: The expository problems in connexion with Hume's theory of religion are of a somewhat different character. His chief work on this subject, the *Dialogues concerning Natural Religion,* was not published in his lifetime. *The Natural History of Religion* was among the last of his philosophical writings: it appeared in 1757. It might be concluded that his interest in the philosophy of religion dated from a comparatively late period. Such a conclusion is in fact quite unjustified: religious philosophy was amongst the earliest of Hume's interests, and may well have antedated his interest in pure morals.

17

Indeed, it is not too much to say that Hume's attitude to religion was one of the chief factors in all his philosophical thinking. His attitude was one of unqualified enmity. The religion of his boyhood was a grim form of Calvinism emphasizing pre-election, guilt, and damnation, and it made a deep impression on his mind. His earliest philosophical activity seems to have been an attempt to remove himself from the power of these unhappy doctrines. His published work and independent testimony concerning his life and character, together testify to the success of this attempt. His tranquillity in the face of death excited the admiration of his friends, the amazement of James Boswell, and the incredulity of Samuel Johnson. But nevertheless, to the very end of his life, the thought of immortality, or of survival after death, was, for him, indissolubly associated with sentiments of terror and dismay.

Hume's works on religion exhibit two distinct lines of argument. In the *Natural History* he sets himself the task of giving an account of the origin of the idea of God, and of the origin of the belief in the existence of gods. This is carried out independently of any consideration of the validity of such beliefs. It might be expected that he would use the methods of analysis elaborated in the *Treatise*, but this he does not do. Instead, he gives a purely anthropological account, which, both in method and in its display of classical learning, reminds one forcibly of the works of Sir James Frazer. The object of the *Dialogues*, on the other hand, is to examine and assess some arguments which have been brought in favour of the existence of God. The argument chiefly considered is the so-called argument from design. This is also the subject of Section 11 of the *Enquiry concerning Human Understanding*. Section 10 of the same work deals destructively with the possibility of miraculous events.

CHAPTER 2

AIMS AND METHODS

WHEN we want to understand a philosopher it is a good plan to ask what were his aims, and what methods did he use to pursue those aims. We cannot take these things for granted in philosophy, as we can in other subjects. The short answer with Hume is that his aims were revolutionary, and that like all revolutionaries he was prepared to use almost any method that presented itself. Of course, this does not mean he was at all disingenuous: he was certainly not prepared to use arguments which he privately considered to be invalid. A more detailed answer is hard to give, partly because Hume seems to have misconceived somewhat the nature of the arguments he in fact used, and partly because his real aims are not at first very clearly stated. Let us first see what he has to say in his *Introduction to the Treatise of Human Nature*.

Hume tells us he is going to study 'the Science of Man', and that the object of this science is 'to explain the principles of human nature'.[1] The method he proposes is 'the experimental method', and this involves the performance of 'careful and exact experiments'. These experiments may include either introspective observation of mental phenomena, or the objective observation of human behaviour. Hume is very cautious about introspection because, he says, 'reflection and premeditation would so disturb the operation of my natural principles, as must render it impossible to form any just conclusion from the phenomenon'. He concludes that 'we must therefore glean up our experiments in this science from a cautious observation of human life ... by men's behaviour in company, in affairs, and in their pleasures'. All this makes it look just as if he is going to do what we should now call experimental psychology. But if we read Hume's works, we do not find any accounts of 'careful and exact experiments', nor do we find any 'cautious observations of men's behaviour'. There is something that Hume calls 'an experiment', but this is a procedure all his own, and it is invariably intro-spective in character. There are observations of human behaviour, but they are not accounts of a particular man's behaviour in carefully specified circumstances. They are accounts of certain general features of human behaviour, which are in fact obvious to everybody.

A different light is thrown on the matter if we consider the motives Hume says he has for investigating human nature. The enquiries are not made just for their own sake, or out of curiosity. There is an ulterior motive. It appears that all the other sciences have a special relation to the science of man, which makes the latter in a certain sense ultimate. Thus Mathematics, Natural Philosophy (that is Physics), and Natural Religion are dependent on the science of man be-cause 'they lie under the cognizance of men, and are judged of by their powers and faculties'. It therefore behoves us to know the extent and nature of these powers and faculties. Logic, Morals, Criticism, and Politics are even more closely connected with human nature because 'the sole end of logic is to explain the principles and operations of our reasoning faculty, and the nature of our ideas; morals and criticism re-gard our tastes and sentiments; and politics consider men as united in society, and dependent on each other.' Hume con-cludes that, in proposing a science of man, he is in effect pro-posing 'a complete system of the sciences, built on a founda-tion almost entirely new, and the only one upon which they can stand with any security'. It is clear that when Hume speaks of a science he means any field of human enquiry, and does not restrict himself to what we should now call a science. So what he is really going to investigate is the *foundation of all human knowledge*.

It is essential for us to understand why Hume thought it important to enquire into the foundations of human know-ledge, for here again it was not just a matter of idle curiosity. He was concerned to destroy, once and for all, an ancient and powerful belief. In his opinion, of course, this belief was false, but that was not the whole of it. He also felt that it was some-how a presumptuous belief, which led to evil consequences by producing in men an unwarrantable pride and intolerance. It seemed too, to have vague associations in his mind with irrational and superstitious fear or anxiety.[2] On the face of it, the belief in question seems harmless enough, even if it is false. It is, to put it shortly, the belief that two quite different kinds of knowledge are possible: an inferior everyday kind of knowledge, and a superior god-like kind of knowledge beside which ordinary knowledge appears as a mixture of error and illusion. Ordinary knowledge, that is the inferior kind, includes all knowledge of matters of fact obtained by observation and experience, and also the systematization of such information in what we now call science. The superior knowledge consists essentially in knowledge of the ultimate *reasons* why things are as they are. We may call the latter metaphysical knowledge, without begging any questions. The acquisition of metaphysical knowledge is supposed, by those who believe in it, to be the proper aim of philosophy.

The possession of metaphysical knowledge is believed by those who seek it to have certain desirable accompaniments. First, the possession of such knowledge, at least in its highest form, entails its permanent retention, and this in turn leads to a state of *eternal happiness*. Since the happiness is eternal, it is clear that metaphysical knowledge must be a key to some form of immortality. Second, knowledge of this kind enables the soul to gain mastery over or freedom from the bodily passions and appetites. These are supposed to be evil, or at best amoral. Consequently moral virtue consists in gaining this mastery, and so it must be a concomitant of metaphysical knowledge. Apart from all this, metaphysical knowledge is usually believed to consist in the contemplation of certain transcendental objects, of which I shall have more to say. It is said that, when we contemplate these objects, we then *see* why things must be as they are. Metaphysical knowledge is acquired by successfully following a certain rational procedure or ritual. This ritual is possible to man because he possesses a supernatural faculty, which we may call the Reason. The Reason is supernatural both in the sense that it is not subject to the accidents which beset the physical body, and in the sense that it is the immortal or eternal or divine part of man.[3]

In view of the powerful associations of such phrases as 'eternal happiness' it is not surprising that these ideas exercise a strong fascination over many minds. If people come to philosophy for help in their search for happiness or freedom or virtue, or even just knowledge of final answers to ultimate questions, they will be both disappointed and annoyed by someone who calls himself a philosopher and yet makes it his business to assure them that the latter demand is impossible to satisfy, and that the former are not to be obtained by the exercise of Reason. Since this is exactly what Hume does, it is no wonder that, although he is admittedly the greatest English-speaking philosopher, he is also commonly regarded as the most exasperating.

Hume says that freedom (in the philosophical sense) is an illusion; he says that we cannot gain happiness and virtue by the exercise of reason alone, because reason alone can never gain mastery over the passions; he says we can never know the ultimate reasons why things are as they are, because the human understanding is not capable of such knowledge. A few quotations will illustrate these, and other points.[4]

We can never free ourselves from the bonds of necessity. We may imagine we feel a liberty within ourselves; but a spectator can commonly infer our actions from our motives and character; and even where he cannot, he concludes in general, that he might, were he perfectly acquainted with every circumstance of our situation and temper.

We speak not strictly and philosophically when we talk of the combat of passion and of reason. Reason is, and ought only to be the slave of the passions, and can never pretend to any other office than to serve and obey them.

When we see, that we have arrived at the utmost extent of human reason, we sit down contented, though we be perfectly satisfied in the main of our ignorance, and perceive that we can give no reason for our most general and most refined principles, beside our experience of their reality; which is the reason of the mere vulgar.

The utmost effort of human reason is to reduce the principles, productive of natural phenomena, to a greater simplicity, and to resolve the many particular effects into a few general causes, by means of reasonings from analogy, experience, and observation. But as to the causes of these general causes, we should in vain attempt their discovery; nor shall we ever be able to satisfy ourselves, by any particular explication of them. These ultimate springs and principles are totally shut up from human curiosity and enquiry.

The observation of human blindness and weakness is the result of all philosophy, and meets us at every turn, in spite of our endeavours to elude or avoid it.

Nothing, therefore, can be more contrary than such a philosophy to the supine indolence of the mind, its rash arrogance, its lofty pretensions, and its superstitious credulity.

There is little need for me to comment on these extracts at present, but we must notice two things. Hume has a theory *and* an attitude. His theory is that the human understanding, or reason, is subject to a limitation, so that there are things we cannot ever know. His attitude is indicated by the fact that he condemns the rather noble aspirations of the ancient philosophers, by implication, as *lofty pretensions*, the outcome of *rash arrogance;* and they are associated with *superstition.* In doing this he is, of course, guilty of some injustice. The opinions of men like Plato, Aristotle, or Spinoza never had the evil consequences which superstitions so often have. It is true that Aristotle's works were used to give a rational basis for a certain kind of Christianity,[5] which Hume would no doubt regard as superstition, and which was in the seventeenth century attended with notable exhibitions of intolerance and persecution. Religious persecution was as close to Hume as political persecution is to us. It is also certainly true that Hume's philosophy could not possibly be used to support any religion or superstition.

We must now try to get some idea of *how* Hume supposes the reason or understanding to be limited, and of what *methods* he uses to establish those limitations. We noticed that perhaps the chief limitation, although not the only one, is

23

that we cannot know the ultimate reasons why things are as they are. We cannot know the ultimate reason why the moon causes the tides, because this would involve somehow seeing that it is *in the nature* of the moon to cause the tides. That is to say, we should be able by examining the moon *alone*, to see why it *must* cause the tides, or at any rate it looks as if this is what we should be able to do. We noticed also that Hume describes his method as an experimental method, involving careful and accurate experiments, and I have warned the reader that this is not a fair description of his actual procedure. Roughly speaking, what Hume does in fact try to do is to show that no possible experience would *constitute* knowledge of ultimate reasons. He tries to establish this, first by showing that no experiences we have on occasions when we might be expected to know ultimate reasons, do in fact constitute such knowledge; and second by showing that we cannot ever imagine anything which we should call experiencing or knowing an ultimate reason. The second point is, of course, the really important and decisive one. Hume proposes to establish the limitation of the human understanding, by establishing a limitation of the human imagination.

It is clear that the imagination will have to be limited in quite a special way, in order to prove Hume's point. A man who has never tasted pineapple cannot imagine that taste, but this does not mean that he can never know what a pineapple tastes like. His imagination is limited by his experience. Again, a man may not be able to imagine something, just because the complexity of the thing defeats, as we say, his imagination. It is clear that such limitations are accidental in character, and cannot be used to prove any absolute and universal restrictions on all human knowledge. They cannot be used to prove that a higher kind of knowledge is impossible for human beings, simply in virtue of the fact that they are human beings. What Hume has to say, and what he does say, is that human experience is of such a kind, and the human imagination works in such a way, that we cannot know or even imagine ultimate reasons.

Even so, it does look at first as if the quarrel between Hume and the old metaphysicians is simply a verbal one. Hume says that certain things are beyond human powers. To prove this, he must establish first that given only such and such powers then these things are impossible, and second that human beings have only such and such powers. If we now define human beings as beings whose powers are limited in the required way, we shall have our second proposition, but it will then be open to the metaphysician to reply that there are no human beings in *this* sense of the phrase. He will say we are all superhuman because our powers are not in fact limited in the way described. Thus it looks as if Hume is bound to establish the limits of the human understanding by a process of cautious generalization from a large number of individual observations and experiments. One pictures the careful examination of a large and fair sample of mankind, the noting of some features common to all the men in the sample, and the extension of these features to all men in general by induction. This is our average picture of scientific procedure, and perhaps Hume really believed at times that he was using some such procedure. But the arguments he actually uses do not follow this simple pattern.

There are really two quite different motives for investigating the limitations of the human understanding, and although Hume seems to have confused them, there is to my mind no doubt which was his principal aim. This may be illustrated by means of an example. No man can leap a distance of fifty feet. Such knowledge of human limitations would be of use to builders of moats round castles: they will know that fifty feet is wide enough. You can imagine economically minded moat-builders carrying out extensive investigations into the athletic powers of soldiers, just to find out the smallest efficient moat. On the other hand, you may tell a man that no one can leap fifty feet, just in order to dissuade him from attempting such a thing. In this case, the general information is not really required: all he needs to know is that *he* cannot leap the distance. Furthermore, whereas the moat-builder really does need for his purpose some scientific knowledge of human limitations in general, the man who wants to confine himself to attempting only those athletic feats which are possible for him, does not need such knowledge. All he requires is a test he can apply to himself, and which will establish for him *his* limitations. Consequently, a man who wants to dissuade people from attempting certain tasks, may proceed in two quite different ways. He may attempt a scientific demonstration that the tasks are beyond all human capacity. Or he may provide a test, which people can apply to themselves, and which (so he believes) will demonstrate to them that the tasks are beyond their capacity. The latter method of dissuasion is unquestionably more effective than the first.

I have suggested that Hume wants to persuade us to abandon the search for a higher kind of knowledge. No really scientific demonstration is required for this purpose. All he needs to do is to lead the reader to see his own limitations. If Hume's works are seen in this light, they make great philosophy and good sense. If they are taken the other way, they look like poor psychology and poor sense. I do not wish to suggest that Hume himself saw it altogether like this, or that I have really succeeded in cramming his philosophy into a nutshell. But what we need, with Hume perhaps above all others, is some sort of clue which will guide us through his works, and enable us to extract some sort of pattern. When we have done this, we may be in a position to reconsider our attitude.

Hume's contention is not that our understanding (that is, our power of acquiring knowledge) is limited in the sense that we are not as clever as we might be. No doubt we are limited in this way, but the limitation Hume seeks to establish is one which would hold no matter how clever or intelligent we are. For him our understanding is limited because our imagination is limited, and our experience is limited. What is more, these limitations are intrinsic and not accidental. That is to say, it is not simply that our imagination is not so strong as it might be, and our experience is not so extensive as it might be. So long as our imagination works in the way it does, and so long as our experience is of the kind it is, the limitations Hume seeks to impose will hold. What we have to explain,

26

then, is what Hume conceives experience to consist of essentially, how he considers the imagination to work, and how these things bear on what we can or cannot know.

It is absolutely central in Hume's philosophy that there can be only one kind of experience. You will notice that here he at once departs from the old metaphysical tradition, in which possession of true knowledge is connected with a special kind of experience, involving the contemplation of a special kind of object. Hume calls the one kind of experience 'perception', and what he means by a perception is close to what we mean by a *sensation*. He says 'to hate, to love, to think, to feel, to see; all this is nothing but to perceive',[6] and he might well have added 'to remember, to expect, to imagine, to believe, to know'. Thus Hume's 'perception' makes a clean sweep. Furthermore, to imagine something is to form a sort of *mental picture* of it, that is, it is a kind of shadowy experience of the real thing. This mental picture, he calls an 'idea'. When we are thinking, it does not necessarily follow that we are having ideas of what we are thinking about, for we may think in words. But in so far as we are really thinking, it follows that we *could* have ideas of what we are thinking about, and these ideas will be mental pictures, that is, shadowy intimations of some possible experience. It follows that *what can be imagined or thought of can also be experienced*. This is the first of Hume's great principles of investigation.

Hume conceives experiences as distinct entities, and he thinks that complex experiences are by us distinguishable into parts. His second principle is that *the parts of a complex experience may be imagined or pictured as existing separately*. His third principle is that *we can never perceive any real connexion between distinct existences*. It is not very clear what Hume means by a real connexion among distinct existences, or what he means by saying we can never perceive such real connexions. But it appears later that an example of a real connexion would be a relation between two objects A and B, such that the existence of A somehow necessitated the existence of B. In any case, it is clear that since by Hume's first principle we cannot imagine what cannot be experienced, it follows that

27

we cannot even imagine a real connexion between distinct existences. The reader will notice that there is something a little puzzling about this conclusion. It looks as if there will be a contradiction in terms when we speak of perceiving real or necessary connexions among distinct existences. And then we wonder how people could have supposed themselves to have perceived something which cannot even be imagined.

In the body of the *Treatise*, Hume uses his principles to accomplish what we may call an *analysis* of certain important ideas. The nature of his analysis is illustrated in the following extracts.[7]

The idea of space or extension is nothing but the idea of visible or tangible points distributed in a certain order.

Time is nothing but the manner in which some real objects exist.

Belief is nothing but a strong and lively idea derived from a present impression related to it.

Necessity is nothing but that determination of the thought to pass from causes to effects, and from effects to causes, according to their experienced union.

[The self] is nothing but a bundle or collection of different perceptions.

We need not concern ourselves at present with the exact meaning of these remarks, nor need we suppose that they adequately represent Hume's final conclusions. We are interested in what is common to them all, and this scarcely needs indicating, for it consists simply in the repeated use of the words 'nothing but'. Hume's formula for analysis is to tell us that Xs are really but Ys, and the implication of this formula is that we had mistakenly supposed that Xs were something more than just Ys. Besides this, there is another suggestion which becomes clear later, and that is the suggestion that we had mistakenly supposed Xs to have a kind of independent existence which they do not in fact have. Thus perhaps, we have taken space and time to be, not merely the manner in which real objects exist, but rather some thing or medium in which objects exist. We are apt to imagine objects existing in space and time, as fish exist in water; and because of this we are inclined to suppose we can imagine space and time continuing to exist independently of the existence of any other objects whatever. In the same way, we think of the self or mind as something which *has* perceptions, or again as something in which perceptions exist. We suppose that perceptions depend for their existence on the prior existence of a mind to perceive them, and consequently that the mind does not depend for its existence on the existence of perceptions. All this suggests to us that there are things which have an independent existence, and which can be imagined as existing separately, and yet which cannot be perceived, at least in the ordinary sense. The purpose of Hume's deflationary kind of analysis is then clear, for he wants to prove that we cannot imagine anything, and so cannot propose the existence of anything which is not a possible object of common experience.

We can now consider very shortly the approximate bearing of Hume's theory of the imagination on his theory of knowledge. The key to the situation is his idea that we can imagine only what can be experienced. One other assumption is needed for a simple exposition, and that is the assumption that knowledge of the existence of something consists primarily in that thing's being an object of present experience. Thus, ignoring certain philosophical irrelevancies, we know in the primary sense that a lion exists if we actually see one at the zoo. It is obvious that, if there are things which are not objects of any possible experience, then we cannot know of their existence, at least in this simple way. If we want to do a little mythical history of philosophy, we may pretend that when metaphysicians spoke of a second kind of experience, this was because they believed both in the existence of unexperienceable objects (sometimes called occult objects), *and* that we can know of the existence of such objects in a way like the way we know lions exist when we see them. This is not the true situation, but it may have been how Hume sometimes saw it. But the effects of his principles are plain enough. First, if there are occult objects, we can never know of their existence. Second, we cannot even imagine occult objects, and cannot, therefore, believe in, assert, deny, doubt, or in any way entertain the existence of such objects. It follows that whenever we suppose ourselves to be entertaining the idea of an occult object, we are really under an illusion, for either there is no idea at all, or it is the idea of something which can occur in common experience. This is surely the strangest of all illusions, the illusion that we believe in the existence of something which cannot even be imagined, and Hume's final task is obviously to explain to us how such illusions arise, and just what they are illusions of. Not unnaturally he finds some difficulty, for it will be the final explanation of how the great fantasy of the old metaphysicians gained its hold over men's minds.

Hume's way of solving this problem is both complicated and obscure, but a few guiding remarks are in place here. We cannot believe in the existence of occult things or qualities, because on his terms you can believe only what you can imagine, and can imagine only what you can experience. Because of this, he says that we *feign* the existence of occult or unperceivable objects,[8] and this is not just his way of avoiding the issue. He then needs to explain, first how we come to feign the existence of such objects, and second what this feigning consists of, for it plainly cannot be the same as believing. In order to accomplish the first of these tasks he finds it necessary to introduce two further basic principles. The first is that, if two ideas are closely associated in some way, we are apt to mistake one for the other. The second is that, if some object arouses a certain feeling in our minds, we are apt to project that feeling onto the object, and to regard it as a real quality of the object. Thus we speak of a sad scene, although the sadness is really in the spectators. We shall see later how these principles are used.

To understand what feigning is, we need to say a little about Hume's theory of meaning. His theory is that primarily the meaning of a word is an idea for which the word stands, or which it represents. Thus the use of a word is determined on this theory by the nature of the idea it stands for, and by using a word to stand for a certain idea, we naturally get into

the habit of using it in a certain way. It comes to occupy a
certain position, so to speak, in our discourse, just because the
corresponding idea has a certain place among other ideas.
Having acquired this habit, it is no longer necessary for us to
picture to ourselves the idea which the word means, when we
wish to use it meaningfully or correctly. In this sense we can
often be quite clear about what we mean, without having a
clear and distinct picture of what we mean; and it is obvious
enough that this often happens. But, according to Hume's
theory, for a word to have a meaning it is not sufficient that
it should have a use: it must also stand for an idea which
determines the use. And this idea is a kind of image or picture
of something which the word represents or means. Thus,
when we use a word meaningfully, we need not have the idea
or meaning before us, so to speak, but it is absolutely necessary that there should be an idea which we could form, and
which would be the meaning of the word.[9]

The process of feigning may now be briefly explained. If a
word has meaning, it must of course be used in a certain way;
but it does not follow that because a word is used in some way,
it must have one and only one meaning. It may have many
meanings, or it may have no meaning at all. The only way to
find out is to track down the idea for which the word stands,
and this entails finding the experience from which the idea is
derived. Philosophers sometimes feel there ought to be a word
having a certain use, and they duly invent one. Then they
think that by giving the word a use they have succeeded in
giving it a meaning, that is to say they have made it stand for
an idea. And then, all too often, it turns out that if the word
does stand for an idea, this must be an idea of something
which can never be experienced. This is one kind of feigning.
On the other hand, a word may have a meaning, or it may
perhaps have two or more closely similar meanings, and here
we can see a possibility of confusion. If a word has many uses,
no single idea will account for all of them, and if we suppose
it must have one and only one meaning, we shall be inclined
to imagine that that meaning must be something more than
the ideas which partly account for its use. Again, if two words

like 'water' and 'space' have somewhat parallel uses, we may imagine that the parallelism extends further than it really does. This will make us think of space as an independently existing entity, just like water, except that it cannot be seen or felt as water can. This is the kind of account Hume gives of how we come to feign the existence of occult things or qualities.

Hume does not explicitly develop the distinction between use and meaning, but in practice he utilizes this distinction. We noticed that he said we sometimes mistake one idea for another, and you will see that this kind of mistake appears altogether mysterious, if not impossible. In practice, however, he demonstrates that we mistake one use of a word for another. Indeed, his way of avoiding such mistakes is to go back to the idea which is the meaning, and this would not accomplish anything if you could also mistake one idea for another.

CHAPTER 3

THE IMAGINATION

I

The Treatise of Human Nature opens with a classification of
what Hume calls 'perceptions of the human mind'. He tells
us that 'everything which appears to the mind is nothing but
a perception', and that 'to hate, to love, to think, to feel, to
see; all this is nothing but to perceive'.[1] Thus hating, loving,
thinking, feeling, and seeing consist of nothing but the
appearance of perceptions to the mind. It is important to
notice that Hume does not argue this point, and this means
he is not setting up a psychological theory about the nature
of hating, loving, and the rest. We should rather regard his
account of these things as definitive of what he means by a
'perception of the human mind'. Now we cannot question a
definition, but we may well ask after its purpose, and Hume's
purpose is not at present clear to us.

Perceptions of the mind are first divided into *impressions* and
ideas. The difference between these 'consists in the degrees of
force and liveliness, with which they strike upon the mind,
and make their way into our thought and consciousness'.[2]
Impressions 'enter with most force and violence', and ideas
are 'the faint images of these in thinking and reasoning'. The
relation between impressions and ideas is further illustrated
in the following passage:[3]

When I shut my eyes and think of my chamber, the ideas I form
are exact representations of the impressions I felt; nor is there any
circumstance of the one, which is not to be found in the other.

The important thing about this passage is again that it is put
forward as an obvious truth which does not call for argument
or other support. Now it would be an obvious truth if we de-
leted 'and think of my chamber' and inserted the words 'and
form a complete and accurate mental picture of my chamber'. So, for Hume, to think of something, or to form an idea

of it, means making an accurate mental picture. It is no wonder then that he goes on to say the first thing that strikes him about ideas, is that they are perfect copies of impressions.[4] For an idea is an idea of just that impression which it exactly reproduces. This is what makes that idea an idea of just that impression.

Impressions, and ideas also, may be further divided into those which are *simple* and those which are *complex*.[5] It is not very clear what Hume has in mind when he speaks of simple impressions, but it is quite clear that he conceives complex impressions to be built up from simple impressions, rather as a house is built of bricks, or as in chemistry a molecule is composed of atoms. Thus simple impressions are the atoms or elementary constituents of our experience, and Hume defines them as 'admitting of no distinction nor separation'. There is no need for any further definition at present, so long as we grasp the fact that Hume's conception is of an experience which can be analysed, or rather discriminated into simple elements, which do not themselves admit of further analysis. It is again important to notice that he does not argue for this view of experience: he presents it as something which must, if understood, meet with immediate acceptance.

The third classification of impressions, and so also of ideas, is the division into impressions of *sense* and impressions of *reflection*.[6] The examples he gives of impressions of reflection are, 'desire and aversion, hope and fear', that is, what we should commonly call feelings or sentiments. They are called impressions of reflection because they arise from reflection on previous experience. The distinction Hume has in mind is that sentiments or feelings or impressions of reflection usually have an object, and this means we hope for something, fear something, and so on. The account he gives of hoping for X, is that to hope for X is to have a feeling or impression of hope which is consequent on or caused by contemplation of the idea of X. It is once more important to notice that this is not presented as a psychological theory about what really happens when we hope for something. No evidence is produced. It is simply that saying you have an impression of hope arising from the idea of X, is presented as *another way of saying* you hope for X. There is no question of the truth of a way of expressing yourself, only a question of its purpose, and whether that purpose is achieved. We do not yet know what Hume's purpose is.

We now come to two propositions which Hume does make some attempt to support by evidence. He says

every simple idea has a simple impression, which resembles it, and every simple impression a correspondent idea.[7]

and

all our simple ideas in their first appearance are derived from simple impressions, which are correspondent to them, and which they exactly represent.

Since Hume has already defined an idea as an exact copy of an impression, it may be supposed that the first of these propositions is already established by definition, but he is now concerned with something that cannot be side-stepped in this way. Someone who is metaphysically inclined can agree that under Hume's definition of an idea, every idea must correspond to some impression, and yet hold that there are objects which are ordinarily called ideas, and which do not correspond to any possible impression. The fact that Hume does not call such things ideas, does not prove that they do not exist; and he cannot show the limitations of the human understanding simply by making a definition. It is here that we should expect the 'experimental method' to be employed.

The proof of universal correspondence between simple impressions and simple ideas falls into three parts: a report, a request, and a challenge. Hume first reports that when he examines the ideas in his own mind, he finds that as a matter of fact in his case every idea is a copy of an impression.[8] He then requests the reader to satisfy himself in a like manner that all his ideas are copies of impressions. Then he challenges anyone who disagrees to *produce* an idea which does not correspond to any possible impression. Since no one answers his challenge, he regards his conclusion as established. It is just as if you undertook to convince a certain group of people that none of them possesses a silver coin. You first examine all the coins in your possession, and find that none of them are silver. Then you ask all the other people to examine their coins. And then you challenge anyone who claims to possess a silver coin to produce it, and if they cannot do so you conclude that they must be mistaken. But there is one important difference between Hume's argument and the argument about the coins; you cannot produce your ideas for public examination, you can produce only words. It looks as if the challenge should really be, to specify in words an idea which does not correspond to any impression.

Now Hume's purpose in proving the principle of correspondence between impressions and ideas is to show us that we are mistaken in supposing that we have certain ideas, and this means we are mistaken in supposing that certain phrases express ideas. For example, Hume says we have no idea of a vacuum or empty space, and likewise no idea of time as something existing independently of change. He says of each of these alleged ideas

whence should it be derived? Does it arise from an impression of sensation or of reflection? Point it out distinctly to us, that we may know its nature and qualities. But if you cannot point out *any such impression*, you may be certain you are mistaken, when you imagine you have any such idea.[9]

Dealing with the notion of power or causal efficacy, he says

all ideas are derived from, and represent impressions. We never have any impression, that contains any power or efficacy. We never therefore have any idea of power.

In these examples it is quite clear that the principle of correspondence between impressions and ideas is used to establish that certain words do not express ideas. So if someone claims that a particular word stands for an idea which corresponds to no possible impression, Hume's answer will be that this cannot be the case, because every idea corresponds to some impression. It is not surprising that he believes there will be no successful answers to his challenge. No matter how he purports to prove his principle, the use he makes of it shows that for him an idea is *by definition* a copy of an impression.

The second principle says that we cannot have any simple idea without previously having had the appropriate simple impression. For example, we cannot form the idea of the taste of pineapple, unless we have already tasted one. Hume gives some other examples, but they add little to the argument, and in some sense the principle seems indisputable. The only point to be noticed, is that in this case it is not a matter of definition, but a matter of fact. An idea is defined as a faint copy of an impression, and there is nothing in this to make one conclude that impressions must always precede ideas. The contrary can be imagined to be true, although it does in fact appear to be false. This second principle is, however, of subsidiary importance only, in so far as it lends a certain additional force to the principle of correspondence between simple impressions and simple ideas. The latter is Hume's chief analytical tool. The fact that it is established by definition, and not by observation, has some important consequences.

We must now consider a little more closely the difference between impressions and ideas.[10] Hume uses many words to describe this difference – strength, force, liveliness, vivacity, are some of them. We might have thought the difference was that impressions are caused by real objects, whereas ideas are not, but Hume does not wish to commit himself to this as a definition. Perhaps there is this difference, but it is not the difference which enables us to know immediately whether we are actually having a sensation of sight, or only thinking of such a sensation. Our knowledge is immediate, and so must be a matter of immediate experience: the nature of the experience must itself tell us whether it is a case of seeing or of sensing. Hume says we know the difference because ideas are fainter than impressions, but we should not take this too literally, for in another place he just says they feel different. All that he really wants to stress is that the difference, whatever it is, is a matter of immediate experience.

37

Hume makes the same sort of distinction between various kinds of ideas.[11] There is an immediately perceptible difference between the ideas of *memory* and those of the *imagination*, and between these and the ideas which constitute *beliefs*. Hume says that ideas of memory are more vivid than those of the imagination. By this, he does not now mean simply that the difference is apparent, but also that memories influence us more than imaginings do. They play a greater part in the determination of our thoughts and actions. There is a troublesome verbal point here, which must be cleared up before we can proceed. On Hume's definition of a memory we can have false memories as well as true ones. On his definition a memory is an idea which has a certain apparent character, and *not* necessarily an idea of something that really happened. Other people would define a memory as an idea of something that really happened, but so long as we realize that this is not Hume's definition, there need be no confusion. Of course, Hume allows that memories under his definition, that is to say ideas having this special character, very often are ideas of something that really happened, but this is not a matter of necessity: it is just a matter of fact, which might well have been otherwise.

Hume's account of belief follows on his account of memory; indeed a memory is one kind of belief. His stock form of belief, so to speak, is a belief in the existence of something, and to believe in the existence of something is to have a specially vivid idea of it. We need not at present go into this in detail, but we may make two observations. First, the characteristic of an idea of belief is that it has a marked influence on our decisions and actions, and this is what really distinguishes it from an idea of the imagination. Second, Hume says that to conceive of something and to conceive of it *as existing* are one and the same operation.[12] There is no separate idea of existence, for existence or reality is not a kind of quality or characteristic which some things happen to possess. For example, the difference between a real horse and an imaginary horse is not at all the same sort of thing as the difference between a race-horse and a cart-horse. A real horse is not a *special kind* of horse. It is one of the advantages of the picture theory of meaning that this point comes out quite clearly. You cannot tell, simply by examining a picture, whether it is a picture of something which really exists. To do this, you have to look about you, and see if there is anything in the world that corresponds to the picture. The correspondence between the picture and reality cannot itself be put into the picture.

This account of existence is very important in Hume's philosophy, and so we may enlarge on it a little. When we say that horses have four legs, we are certainly saying that horses have a particular feature in common, but it is plausible to suppose we are saying something more than this. We can suppose that the possession of four legs is one of the *essential* features of a horse. A thing cannot be a horse unless it has four legs. Even if it was in other respects very much like a horse, if it had three legs, or five legs, it would not be a proper horse, but some kind of monster. Now, there have been philosophers who have thought of existence as a characteristic possessed by some things, just like four legs; and this seems to have led them to entertain the notion that there might be things one of whose *essential* features is existence. If this were so, there would be things which necessarily exist, just as horses necessarily have four legs. It was supposed, for example, that the existence of God could be proved by showing that existence was part of his essence, which is to say existence is one of the essential features of God. The argument ran roughly as follows: God is, by definition, perfect, and one of the characteristics essential to perfection is existence. Therefore God exists.[13] Hume's reply is that existence is not a characteristic, and so it cannot be one of the characteristics essential to perfection. So the proof (which is sometimes called the Ontological Proof of the existence of God) must fail.

In Hume's theory, we can never have an idea of something which necessarily exists, because for him an idea is a kind of picture, and it is perfectly obvious that nothing in a picture makes it necessary that what it is a picture of should exist. Once we grasp this, it is easy to see at least one of the mistakes in the ontological proof. And it is fairly easy to see that treating existence on all fours with other predicates really is a mistake, even if Hume's picture theory of ideas is itself wrong. What his theory does, and this is a point in its favour, is to bring out the difference between existence and qualities with unusual clearness. But if Hume is right, it becomes hard to understand how the confusion ever arose. We shall return to this point when we come to discuss Hume's attitude to religion. All we need for the present are the two general observations, that existence is not a quality, and that nothing exists of necessity. If we want to know whether horses, or anything else, exists, we must look and see.

It would seem from Hume's account that believing in the existence of horses is the same as believing that there are objects corresponding to an idea we have, namely, the idea we call an idea of a horse. But this is not what he says. For him, to believe in the existence of something is simply to have a vivid idea of it, in his special sense of 'vivid'. In the *Enquiry concerning Human Understanding* he explains the matter as follows:[14]

Belief is nothing but a more vivid, lively, forcible, firm, steady conception of an object, than what the imagination alone is ever able to attain. This variety of terms, which may seem so unphilosophical, is intended only to express that act of the mind, which renders realities, or what is taken for such, more present to us than fictions, causes them to weigh more in the thought, and gives them a superior influence on the passions and imagination. Provided we agree about the thing, it is needless to dispute about the terms.

Belief is something felt by the mind, which distinguishes the ideas of the judgement from the fictions of the imagination. It gives them more weight and influence; makes them appear of greater importance; enforces them in the mind; and renders them the governing principle of our actions.

Were we to attempt a *definition* of this sentiment, we should, perhaps, find it a very difficult, if not an impossible task; in the same manner as if we should endeavour to define the feeling of cold or passion of anger, to a creature who never had any experience of these sentiments.

There is a certain sense of stress and dissatisfaction in these passages, and this has two sources. The first is the picture theory of thought and imagination, which we have seen to be the basis of Hume's account. This theory invites, if it does not command, the notion that believing consists essentially in believing that some idea we have represents, or corresponds to, reality (as we have already observed). For if someone asks, of a painted picture: Do you believe this picture? we know they must mean: Do you accept this picture as an accurate representation of some real thing or event? Now one of the ways whereby we come to accept or reject a painted picture, is by comparing it with what we already know or believe concerning the objects or events in question. But we cannot take this way with ideas, considered as mental pictures, because then acceptance of one idea will involve comparing it with another idea, already accepted; and acceptance of this second idea will involve comparison with yet a third idea, and so on indefinitely. There will, in short, be a vicious infinite regress. It follows that mental pictures cannot stand in the same relation to their objects as do painted pictures. Consequently, Hume's account of how we come to acquire the beliefs we do, must be very different from our account of how we come to believe painted pictures, as indeed it is.

The second source of stress, and a much more serious one, is Hume's suggestion that the sole difference between beliefs and ideas of the imagination consists in a feeling which attaches to the former and not to the latter. He speaks as if belief were a certain quality that some ideas have, and others not. And in one of the passages quoted, he compares this feeling with the feeling of cold, or the passion of anger. Now, if we say we believe a painted picture, we commit ourselves to a comparison of the picture with reality, if that is available; and this will decide whether our belief is true or false, for the correctness of a painted picture does undeniably consist in its correspondence to whatever it is supposed to represent. Consequently, if we accept this aspect of the picture theory, when we say we believe that so and so, we are committing ourselves to a comparison of our idea (the idea that so and so) with existing fact; and this is what makes our belief true or false. But if, as Hume suggests, when we say we believe that so and so, we mean only that we have the idea that so and so, and that this idea has some peculiar quality, it is hard to see how we are committing ourselves. It is never self-contradictory to to say: This idea has this feeling (vivid, impressive, what you like), and yet I do not believe it. If ideas are like pictures, they can never claim of themselves to be true or false, any more than pictures can: it is people who make this claim about them. Even if a picture had something immensely impressive about it, so that all who saw it were constrained to believe in the actual occurrence of what was represented, nonetheless this power in the picture would not *constitute* the belief.

Belief is really an attitude which people have, and not a quality possessed by ideas. Hume was perfectly well aware of this, but he wanted to make the attitude a consequence of the quality. In the passages previously quoted, he says that possession of this quality by ideas 'causes them to weigh more in the thought, and gives them a superior influence on the passions and imagination', and 'makes them appear of greater importance; enforces them on the mind; and renders them the governing principle of our action.' It is this superior influence, this controlling power, which constitutes the essence of belief; not the hypothetical quality of which these are supposed to be consequences. We may well ask what led Hume to introduce this hypothetical quality, as a step in explaining the origin of beliefs, for it seems quite superfluous. He wants an explanation of how we come to believe some things, and not others; that is, he wants an explanation of how some ideas come to govern our actions, and some not. He proceeds by explaining how some ideas come to have this peculiar feeling or quality, and then says that ideas with this quality are thereby endowed with the power to govern our actions. It is clear that the feeling or quality serves no useful purpose here: he might just as well have stated that ideas which arise in certain ways do in fact govern our actions, and are in that sense beliefs. It may be said that the quality serves to explain how the ideas govern our actions, but this is a misconception, and entirely contrary to the spirit of Hume's philosophy. No quality or feeling attaching to ideas can entail that they will influence conduct, any more than a quality attaching to real objects can entail that they will cause any particular effects.

There are several possible reasons why Hume was led to take this seemingly inconsistent step, and one, at least, has the advantage of being specific. We have seen that one of the fundamental principles of Hume's philosophy is the theory that the meaning of a word is nothing but the idea which it expresses. For Hume, the meaning of a word is not its use, but something that determines its use, namely an idea. His other principle is that every idea must correspond to some possible impression, and that we cannot have a simple idea unless we have already had the simple impression that corresponds to it. We have seen in general how he uses these principles to establish that certain words either have no meaning at all, or that they do not have the meaning we, as it were, attribute to them in unreflecting moments. He proves his case by showing that the word in question cannot stand for an idea, because there is no possible corresponding impression. It is not too much to say that the whole of Hume's philosophy rests on these two principles, and on their application in the manner described. Now 'belief' is a noun, and is meaningful, and so it must stand for some idea, and this idea must correspond to some impression. Consequently, a belief must consist of an idea somehow linked with an impression, and it would seem that this impression must be the impression of belief. Hume feels, but does not explicitly recognize the need for an impression of belief, and this is what makes him speak of a 'feeling', which is indefinable, like 'the feeling of cold or passion of anger'.

This explanation is, of course, conjectural; and if it is to be convincing, we have to explain why Hume never explicitly admitted an impression of belief. At the beginning of the *Treatise* belief is identified with the force and vivacity of ideas; then comes the notion that the real function of this force and vivacity is to influence conduct. In an appendix to the *Treatise* he introduces the notion that ideas differ in feeling, as well as in force and vivacity, and this feeling is identified with belief in the *Enquiries*. Finally this feeling of belief is indirectly and

43

somewhat obscurely connected with ordinary feelings, like cold and anger. He never gets to the point of saying belief is an impression, just as cold and anger are impressions. It is hard to see why he should fend off the obvious consequence of his own principles in this way. I cannot give any plausible explanation: various possibilities can be suggested, but since all these are inadequate, we need not bother with them here. But we shall return to the point at a later stage.

The general reasons which led Hume to this definition of belief are, as might be expected, largely considerations of convenience. In discussing the origins of beliefs, it is useful to keep discussion in the mental sphere, so as to avoid irrelevant complications, like the mind-body problem. He also claims to define belief as 'an idea associated with a present impression', but this is misleading, for he does not use the proposition as a definition, but as an empirical fact about beliefs.

II

We have seen that Hume's theory of impressions and ideas, and of the connexion between them, is not so much a psychological theory to be verified by observation, as an attempt to provide a framework for analysis. It is more like a system of measurement than a physical theory. And there cannot be any question of the truth of a system of measurement, but only a question of its value or usefulness for some purpose. This is independent of any opinion Hume himself may have had about the absolute validity of his scheme. Cartesian coordinates do not provide the only possible frame of reference for events in physical space, although Descartes may have thought they did. In a like manner, Hume's impressions and ideas do not provide the only possible frame of reference for events in the mental world; and, indeed, attacks on Hume, although they have often had the outward appearance of questioning the psychological validity of his scheme, have invariably been directed at its alleged explanatory inadequacy. Two of Hume's purposes have now become apparent to us. First, he sets up a method for analysis of meaning, in order to show that certain words either have no meaning at all or that they seem to mean more than they really do. Second, he wants to explain how we come to believe some things and not others, or at least to give a plausible account of this process. We now have to consider some further attributes of perceptions of the mind, which bear particularly on the latter of these two objectives.

In the early part of the *Treatise*, Hume makes the following observations.[15] He says that 'everything which appears to the mind is nothing but a perception', that perceptions are 'interrupted and dependent on the mind', that they are 'internal and perishing existences', and that they 'must necessarily appear in every particular what they are, and be what they appear'. Now the second, third, and fourth of these statements do not obviously follow from the first; and since we have taken the first as a definition, the others cannot be taken as definitions, unless the existence of perceptions is accepted as a difficult empirical problem, not to be decided by immediate inspection. Since Hume obviously regards the existence of perceptions as open to determination by immediate inspection, the other statements must be empirical, no matter what private opinions he may have had about them. They must function as statements of fact in his scheme, not as definitions.

When Hume says that perceptions are 'interrupted and dependent on the mind', and are 'internal and perishing existences', he clearly intends us to understand that perceptions cease to exist when unperceived, that there is no such thing as an unperceived perception. And, although I have suggested that his attitude is not wholly consistent, there is no doubt that his final view is that this is a matter of fact. He thinks it is perfectly conceivable that perceptions should continue to exist unperceived, but that in fact they do not. In this respect he is sharply distinguished from his predecessor George Berkeley, who maintained that it is inconceivable for perceptions to continue to exist unperceived.[16] Some explanation of this divergence seems to be required, and may help to clarify Hume's position.

Someone may say that a soldier ceases to exist when he

45

leaves the army, and this is recognized as a picturesque way of saying that anyone who leaves the army ceases to be a soldier, since being a soldier consists simply in having a certain relation to an army. Evidently, one may say in the same sense that perceptions cease to exist when they are not perceived, meaning simply that anything which is no longer perceived is not a perception. In this sense it is logically true that there are no unperceived perceptions, just as it is logically true that every soldier is in an army. But when someone says that soldiers cease to exist when they leave the army, he may not have this logical truth in mind at all. He could be entertaining the fantastic notion that soldiers were completely annihilated on being discharged. This idea, although fantastic, is not logically impossible, for we can conceive of it happening, and it is plainly something much more than just ceasing to be a soldier. I think it is something like this that Hume, and Berkeley for that matter, had in mind when they spoke of perceptions ceasing to exist when unperceived. They meant that, whatever perceptions are, they are completely annihilated when we no longer have them.

The difference between Hume and Berkeley is a consequence of the fact that this analogy between soldiers and perceptions breaks down in one important respect. The way we decide whether or not soldiers are annihilated when they leave the army is the way of experience. We watch what happens to them. If we can still see and touch them after they have received their discharge, we conclude they are not annihilated. If they vanish mysteriously, we conclude that they are annihilated. But we cannot watch what happens to perceptions after we have ceased to perceive them: it is a matter of logic, not a matter of fact, that what is no longer perceived is no longer perceived. At first, then, it seems that Berkeley is right when he suggests that, just as it might be a matter of fact that soldiers are annihilated on discharge, so it is a matter of necessity that perceptions are annihilated when unperceived. But a moment's consideration shows us that this is not an accurate view of the situation. More correctly, we utilize the difference between soldiers and perceptions to suggest

46

(but not to prove) that 'is perceived' and 'exists' should be used interchangeably when applied to perceptions. That is to say, we suggest that saying a perception is perceived should mean simply that it exists. One result of our accepting this suggestion will be that either 'is perceived' or 'exists' or both, do not mean the same when applied to perceptions, as they do when applied to soldiers. For we have observed that to say a soldier is perceived, does not simply mean that he exists.

Further discussion of the question of the independent existence of perceptions is apt to be difficult, but we shall return to it at a later point. Perhaps the origin of the problem lies in a confusion of two different images of the nature of the mind, and of perception. For some people, including Berkeley, the strongest image is that of the mind as a sort of fluid medium, like water, in which perceptions exist as waves do in water. And of course the existence of the waves depends on the prior existence of the water. It does not make sense to talk of the wave leaving the water, unless we mean simply that the wave has ceased to exist. The other image consists of viewing the mind as an organization, like an army. Then perceptions exist in the mind as soldiers do in an army. And here, the existence of the army depends on the prior existence of soldiers, or of entities capable of becoming soldiers. In the one case, perceptions depend for their existence on the existence of a mind; and in the other case the mind depends for its existence on the existence of perceptions. It was this latter kind of image which was uppermost in Hume's thought.

The fourth point Hume makes about perceptions is that 'they must necessarily appear in every particular what they are, and be what they appear.' He does not make much use of this characteristic, although in later theories of perception it came to have a primary importance. What seems to be meant is that our descriptions of our perceptions cannot ever be mistaken, at least in the ordinary sense. In this way perceptions are sharply distinguished from material objects, for the latter certainly do not always appear as they really are. Of course, we can make a sort of mistake about perceptions, even if they do appear as they are. For example, if we are trying to talk French, and have an inadequate grasp of that language, we may see something blue, and describe it as *vert*, under the mistaken idea that *vert* is the French word for blué. But this is different from the mistake we make when we see some real object which appears, as we say, blue to us, and then it turns out that it is really green. It is this latter kind of mistake that Hume supposes we cannot make about our perceptions.

There are two other alleged characteristics of perceptions, which do not appear in the extracts quoted, but which Hume seems on the whole to assume. The first is the idea that perceptions cannot change. For example, if we see a red circle, and it changes (as we say) to green, it would be more proper to say that one perception, a red one, has been replaced by another distinct perception, a green one. The other supposed feature is that perceptions are private, that is to say no two different people can have identically the same perception. People may indeed have perceptions which are exactly alike in all respects, but they will be distinct perceptions, because the people are distinct. It is rather like saying two people cannot perform identically the same action, although of course they can perform exactly similar actions.

To sum up: (1) a perception is anything that 'appears to the mind', (2) perceptions exist only when they appear to the mind, (3) they are just as they seem, (4) they cannot change, (5) they are private. Hume takes all these features of perceptions for granted, except (2), for which he presents an argument. It is tempting to take what he says as a definition of what he means by 'perception', but this leads to the seemingly empirical question, whether there exists any thing which satisfies the definition.

Hume introduces the word 'perceive' in the course of what appears to be another definition, when he says 'to hate, to love, to think, to feel, to see; all this is nothing but to perceive.'[17] And he clearly implies that hearing, touch, taste, and smell are in the same case. Now if we ignore the passions for the present, and consider only the five senses, it seems that the objects of sight, hearing, and the rest, must be perceptions. If this is so, it is necessary to ask whether the objects of the five senses do in fact possess the five characteristics listed in the previous paragraph. And to answer this question, we must first decide what sort of things are objects of the five senses. Unfortunately there are two different answers to this last question. One answer is that what we see are sights, what we hear are sounds, what we smell are smells, and so on. This is true, but not very informative. The other answer is that what we see are material objects, reflections, shadows, and many other things; what we hear are bells, railway trains, thunderclaps; what we smell are roses, garbage; and so on. The exact connexion between these two answers is somewhat puzzling, but there is only one thing we need notice for the present. If the second answer is taken, tables and chairs, reflections, shadows, bells and railway trains, roses and garbage, will all be perceptions. Consequently, if perceptions do really have the five characteristics mentioned, then all these things will have those characteristics. Any such conclusion is bound to evoke some measure of incredulity. Hume is bound to explain himself very fully on this point.

We have considered at some length Hume's classification of perceptions, the properties he attributes to these entities, and some of the objects that might conceivably rank as perceptions. Our immediate object has been to ascertain, at least approximately, what he means when he speaks of perceptions. But it is most important to realize that our ultimate aim in establishing his meaning is *not* to enable us to recognize a Humean perception, if we ever have one; nor is it to decide whether there are such things. It is necessary to stress this, because in the ordinary way when someone uses an unfamiliar noun, or a familiar noun in an uncommon sense, our object in seeking to understand him, is just to be able to recognize what he is referring to, or to ascertain its existence, or to find out whether it really has the properties he says it has. For example, if someone uses the word 'axolotl', we feel that we understand him when we find out how to identify axolotls. That is our object in demanding an explanation of the meaning of 'axolotl'. After we have got this clear, we can

49

go on to verify the existence of axolotls, whether they are, as he says, oviparous, and so on. We know the meaning when we can identify the object at sight. But in many other cases the problem of meaning is not so simple. If you ask a physicist what a quantum is, he cannot tell you how to recognize a quantum when you see it. He may give you a definition, but it will not be at all like a definition of an axolotl. Unless you are very naïve, you will soon come to see that you cannot understand the word 'quantum' without learning some physics (and you can understand 'axolotl' without learning zoology). You understand 'quantum' when you grasp the function of quanta in the explanatory theories of physics. And the question of the existence of quanta is not a question of finding them, but it is a question of the adequacy and the inherent plausibility of physical theories. Hume's theories are not exactly like physical theories, and so the role of his perceptions is not quite analogous to the role of quanta, but the parallel is sufficient for our point. The problem about Hume's perceptions is the problem of their function in his theories: it is not a question of recognizing them, or of picking them out from a lot of other things. But we must remember that, although the object of Hume's theories sometimes appears to be that of scientific explanation, it is not really so.

The first use Hume makes of perceptions is to give an account of how one thing comes to remind us of another.[18] More generally, he wants to explain how thinking, and even imagining, follows a more or less orderly sequence; and it is essential for his ultimate purpose that the explanation should not introduce any rational faculty of the mind, which is supposed by some to impose an external order on our thinking. He therefore asserts that the order is the result of a connexion among ideas, called *association*. If, when you think of X, you are reminded of Y, then in Hume's terms the idea of X is associated with the idea of Y. Likewise, if seeing X reminds you of Y, then the impression of X is associated with the idea of Y. Hume supposes, although he does not explicitly state, that if the idea of X is associated with the idea of Y, then the impression of X is also associated with the idea of Y, and conversely. This supposition appears to accord with the facts, for it is a fact that if thinking of X reminds us of Y, then seeing X reminds us, perhaps even more strongly of Y.

It is not clear whether Hume intends his notion of *association of ideas* to be explanatory or descriptive, but on the whole we may take it as descriptive only. That is, saying the idea of X is associated with the idea of Y, is just a way of saying X reminds us of Y. It is not meant to explain why X reminds us of Y, and not, say, of Z. We still need an explanation why some ideas are associated, and not others. To this end Hume introduces three *principles of association*, which he calls *resemblance*, *contiguity* in space and time, and *cause and effect*. He gives the following examples: (1) Resemblance: a picture naturally leads our thoughts to the original; (2) Contiguity: the mention of one apartment in a building naturally introduces inquiry or discourse concerning the others; (3) Cause and effect: if we think of a wound, we can scarcely forbear reflecting on the pain which follows it. These, although not very well chosen for his purpose, serve to give a rough notion of what is intended.

One or two further points deserve attention. The first is that association of ideas is the result of experience. If we have seen Smith and Jones, who resemble one another, then Smith reminds us of Jones; if we have always met Smith in the company of Jones, then Smith reminds us of Jones; if we have been wounded and felt pain, then wounds remind us of pain. Translated into Hume's terminology, all this is put as follows. If we have had impressions X and Y, which resemble one another, then the idea of X is associated with the idea of Y; if we have had impressions X and Y together, then the idea of X is associated with the idea of Y; if we are aware of a causal connexion between impressions X and Y, then the idea of X is associated with the idea of Y. We notice that in this account, impressions are often tacitly identified with material objects and events in the physical world. The second point is that Hume does not prove that these are the only principles of association, but reports that he has been unable to discover any others. In fact he omits one obvious associating relation, namely logical consequence, but this is not a serious omission from his point of view. The third point is that he specifically states that association does not completely determine a train of thought. It exercises a gentle guidance, rather than a rigid control. Evidently he is here concerned to preserve some element of freedom in our thinking, and he wants this freedom to be a kind of lawlessness or arbitrary irregularity. Any such thing is entirely contrary to his real aims, and in fact he pushes the association of ideas to its limit.

The principles of association of ideas are utilized, not only to explain how one thing reminds us of another, and how our train of thinking comes to have some sort of order, but also to explain how we come to believe some things and not others.[19] We have seen that a fundamental definition of a belief is an idea which exercises a certain influence on conduct; and connected with this, we have Hume's theory that what enables an idea to influence conduct is some quality of the idea, which he calls force or vivacity, and which he does not undertake to define more closely. We have further noted Hume's statement that a belief is 'an idea associated with a present impression', and we are now in a position to understand the meaning and purpose of this. What he means is that, if an idea is associated with an impression which we now have, the idea is naturally called to mind, and furthermore it is endowed with a force, which it would not otherwise have, and which enables it to influence our conduct in the appropriate way. It is as if some of the power of the impression were transferred to the associated idea. This is Hume's account of the genesis of beliefs.

We must now try to see what sort of phenomena Hume is describing in these terms. The principles of translation we have suggested, indicate that he had in mind something like this: if you have always seen Smith and Jones together, and now you see Smith but not Jones, you will be reminded of Jones, and furthermore you will be inclined to think that Jones is somewhere around, even though he is not at present visible. Seeing Smith, you naturally expect to see Jones. This is not an inference so much as a natural expectation. Similarly, if you have found that lightning causes thunder, and you see lightning, you naturally think of the associated thunder, and indeed expect its occurrence. This is how contiguity and causality generate beliefs, or more properly, expectations. It all seems simple and straightforward enough, and more or less in accordance with the facts. There are, however, two anomalous cases which deserve mention. First, not all principles of association serve to generate beliefs. In particular, association of ideas which is the result of resemblance does not so serve. If you see a picture, you may be reminded of the original, but you hardly expect to see the original. Second, there are beliefs which do not appear to be generated by this process. Memories are a kind of beliefs, but we do not believe our memories because they are associated with any present impression. A memory may, of course, be brought to mind by some present experience, with which it is associated, but this is not what makes us believe it. This follows from the fact that memories may also be called to mind by association with some element in a train of imaginative thinking, where there is no direct link with present experience. These exceptions are not of great importance from Hume's point of view, because his object is not really to give an account of beliefs in general, but rather of that special class of beliefs, ordinarily called expectations.

Although in this discussion contiguity in place and time, and cause and effect are treated as distinct principles of association, we shall find later that Hume proposes to establish a very close connexion between them. A somewhat complex argument is used to show that contiguity is primitive, and that causality is a dependent principle. This argument will be fully considered in the next chapter, when its purpose has been made clear. There is, however, one other matter which must be raised, namely Hume's distinction between natural and philosophical relations. I have kept this until last, partly because it is so cryptically expressed that any interpretation must be conjectural, and partly because its value is open to question. Hume introduces the distinction as follows: [20]

The word Relation is commonly used in two senses considerably different from each other. Either for that quality, by which two ideas are connected together in the imagination, and the one naturally introduces the other, after the manner above-explained; or for that particular circumstance, in which, even upon the arbitrary union of two ideas in the fancy, we may think proper to compare them. In common language the former is always the sense, in which we use the word, relation; and 'tis only in philosophy, that we extend it to mean any particular subject of comparison, without a connecting principle.

It seems at first that both natural and philosophical relations are relations between *ideas*. It seems also that the only natural relation between ideas is association, and that all other relations come under the head of philosophical. But when Hume comes to specify these relations, he speaks of *objects*, not of ideas. It is clear that the objects cannot be ideas, from the examples he gives: fire and water, heat and cold (not the ideas of fire and water, heat and cold). These objects may possibly be identified with impressions, but not with ideas. Now it can be suggested that any relation between objects may also be a relation between the ideas of those objects, although this is in itself very dubious. But the associative relation between ideas is not a possible relation between objects: it is indeed produced by certain relations between objects, but there is no theory of association of objects or impressions, corresponding to the theory of association of ideas. The most obvious conclusion is that a natural relation is a relation between ideas, namely association, which does not hold between objects, although it may be produced by certain relations between objects. A philosophical relation is then any relation between objects, which may be paralleled by a corresponding relation between the ideas of those objects. But this is hard to reconcile with Hume's assertion that 'in common language the former (natural relation) is always the sense, in which we use the word, relation'; and with his further assertion that the causal connexion is *both* a natural and a philosophical relation. It seems to me that, on the whole, he meant by a natural relation both the association of ideas and also any relation capable of producing such association. And by a philosophical relation he meant any relation between objects, whether or not it produced an association of ideas. Thus association will be natural but not philosophical; causal connexion and the like will be both natural and philosophical; and other relations (above, heavier than, and the like) will be philosophical only. The only really important point is that the causal connexion is both natural, in so far as it produces association, and philosophical, in so far as it is a relation between objects.

The question of philosophical relations between ideas is extremely puzzling. It does seem that one idea can occur after another, just as one physical event occurs after another (or impressions, if these are identified with observed physical things and events). It seems with rather less plausibility that one idea (in the sense of mental picture) may be lighter in colour than another, as with physical things. But can two ideas be spatially related, or causally connected, as physical things can? We may, of course, imagine two chairs side by side, and we may, if we so wish, speak of this as two ideas of chairs side by side. But they will not be side by side in physical space, or in real space, but rather in what we might call ideal space. Luckily it is not our present business to solve this problem.

CHAPTER 4

THE UNDERSTANDING

I

HUME's theory of knowledge has always been regarded as the most important part of his work. His aim was to make people see the ancient problem of human knowledge in a new light, and he certainly succeeded in doing this. Few subsequent philosophers have had the temerity to do epistemology without 'taking account of Hume', although it is often rather doubtful if the account they took was quite what Hume himself had intended. In the same way, many contemporary philosophers are heavily indebted to Hume both for their problems and for their methods of working, but it is again doubtful if Hume would have collected the debt with much enthusiasm. The fact is that, although Hume managed to work a revolution in philosophical thought, it was not quite the revolution he wanted. I shall not try to account for this just now, or explain it further, but the reader will do well to bear it in mind in what follows.

One way of looking at Hume's theory of knowledge is to divide it into two parts, a criticism of previous theories, and the construction of his own positive theory. But we must be careful here not to misunderstand the nature of his criticism, for it is not directed simply against certain proposed solutions of the old problem of knowledge (whatever that may be) to show that they are false. His aim is rather to show that all solutions of a certain kind are not exactly false so much as impossible or incomprehensible. This process of undercutting the whole subject, problem and answers alike, naturally has a profound influence on the nature of his own positive theory. Evidently it will have to be something quite other than a new solution of the old problem, for the problem itself will have suffered a change. So we find that in his constructive theory, Hume does not seem to occupy himself with the question: How is knowledge possible? nor even with the more radical

56

question: Is knowledge possible? Instead of this we find him attempting to give what appears to be nothing more than a factual account of how certain beliefs are produced in the human mind. Now it is obvious that knowledge and belief are closely related one to the other, but it is very hard to see how a description of the origin of the latter can be a satisfactory solution of philosophical doubts about the possibility of the former, no matter how much those doubts may have been transformed by ingenious criticism. This, then, is the hard part of Hume's theory about the human understanding.

Our first task is to get some idea of what it was that philosophers in general before Hume understood by 'the problem of knowledge'. What difficulties did they imagine to exist? The situation was a little complicated, but a complete survey is not required for our purpose. All we need to grasp is three outstanding characteristics of seventeenth-century philosophy. In the first place, the seventeenth century was remarkable for the rapid and successful development of the empirical sciences – chemistry, physics, and astronomy. Most of us know the great names of this period: Galileo, Kepler, Halley, Newton, Descartes, Leibniz, Harvey, Boyle, Mayow – the list may be prolonged almost indefinitely. And for every one of these there were scores of minor discoverers. If you take any elementary book of science, the names you find in it, Snell, Torricelli, Huygens, Romer, Mercator, and the like, are nearly all seventeenth-century names. To such men we owe, not only our knowledge of basic scientific facts and laws, but also most of the essential tools of experimental science – telescope, microscope, thermometer, barometer, micrometer, calculating machine, and pendulum clock. A miscellaneous list of discoveries can be equally astonishing – the velocity of light, circulation of the blood, gravitation, analytical geometry, infinitesimal calculus.[1]

This is not the place to assess the impact of scientific progress on philosophers, but one point must be observed. This was an entirely new and very powerful kind of knowledge, and so it naturally attracted the attention of those professional lovers of wisdom. Moreover, many of the

57

scientists were consciously proud of their achievement, and were inclined to write prefaces in which they expounded and praised 'the experimental method', and cast scorn on methods which they attributed more or less vaguely to others. Their scorn was not altogether unjustified, for many people had claimed to arrive at the same sort of knowledge, without undertaking the necessary experiments and observations. But the point is that these scientists were very conscious of employing a 'new method', and it was not unnatural to feel that a refinement and codification of this method would aid and secure the advance of scientific knowledge, the wisdom of the future.

If philosophers (who were not always distinct from the scientists) had confined their attention to the codification and refinement of the new scientific method, all would have been well. No harm can come of this useful, if humble, aim. In fact, the titles of some philosophical works of this period give one the impression that this is what is being done. We have the *Rules for the Direction of the Mind* and the *Discourse on Method* of Descartes, and the *Improvement of the Understanding* of Spinoza. The *Discourse on Method* is an introduction to some scientific works of Descartes. But we soon see our impression is a false one, for the philosophers were the inheritors of a quite different and far grander aim, an aim that has little to do with the advancement of science.

This was nothing less than the acquisition of divine or perfect knowledge, as opposed to ordinary fallible human knowledge. The origin of the concept of perfect knowledge, which is of such immense importance in the history of philosophy, is very obscure to us.[2] It is to be found in the earliest speculations of which we have any account, and at first it was supposed that such knowledge was restricted to the gods, and not accessible to human beings. But at a quite early stage philosophers began to think that absolute or perfect knowledge might be within man's compass, a development which was naturally associated with any doctrine asserting the essentially divine or supernatural character of man. Now perhaps at first it was thought that in the new method of science mankind had at last discovered the road to perfect knowledge, but it soon became apparent that mistakes can be made in science as elsewhere, and, moreover, the nature of the reasoning which goes from particular facts to universal statements of law is by no means obvious. So the philosophers ran on to form the idea of a perfect, an infallible method of inquiry, a method which (if correctly used) must be incapable of leading the inquirer into error. They made it their business to show that the new method of science, with perhaps certain emendations and extensions, could be used to obtain the absolute and final knowledge which is the traditional goal of philosophy.

These ideas received a strong impetus from a rather unexpected quarter, namely the development of pure mathematics and of formal logic. It seemed, and it still does seem to many people, that the truths of mathematics are both more durable, and known with greater certainty, than ordinary matters of fact or natural laws. The exact nature and origin of this belief is exceedingly difficult to determine, but however that may be, the belief itself has exerted the profoundest influence on the course of philosophical speculation. The laws of mathematics are described as eternal and necessary, whereas matters of fact are fleeting and contingent. The laws of nature are perhaps eternal, but as we see them they do not appear to share the necessary character of mathematics. It is said we could conceive of a change in the laws of nature, but not in mathematics. Thus, in our knowledge of mathematical truths, we do seem to possess something which approaches the absolute and divine knowledge which philosophers desire. They would like to put all our knowledge, including our knowledge of matters of fact and of the laws of nature, on a similar footing. And this would involve coming to see these things as really necessary and eternal.

Two features of seventeenth-century philosophy have now emerged. Philosophers took as their aim the perfection and justification of the new methods used for the discovery of the laws of nature. For their model of a perfect and justified method, they looked to the processes of mathematical investigation. Now, although progress in mathematics is historically linked with progress in the empirical sciences, the methods employed by mathematicians are *prima facie* quite different from those used by other scientists. The mathematician does not make it his business to perform experiments and 'observe the phenomena': like the philosopher, he just sits and thinks. Perhaps the oldest example of the systematic acquisition of mathematical knowledge is the geometry of Euclid. In this system certain propositions of a general nature, called *axioms*, are first laid down; and then other propositions, called *theorems*, are obtained from these by a process called *deductive inference*. The setting out of such a process, which usually consists of several steps, is called *proof*. The whole method of proving theorems from axioms may well be called the *method of proof*. This method of proof has been extended with great success to many other branches of mathematics, and to formal logic. Indeed, the part it plays in the development of these subjects is very much like the part played by the experimental method in the development of the empirical sciences.[3]

It is obvious that, if the method of proof is to give us a specially secure kind of knowledge, it must satisfy at least two conditions. First, the axioms must be true, since all else depends on them. Second, the process whereby theorems are got from the axioms must preserve the characteristic of truth in the theorems. There is no point in having true axioms if you allow yourself to draw false conclusions from them. The problem of establishing these two conditions is nowadays called the problem of *consistency*, and in its most general form it is a very difficult problem indeed.[4] But in the seventeenth century it does not seem to have been considered at all *as a problem*. For this reason, accounts of the nature of mathematical knowledge are apt to be perfunctory. An explanation (if it can be so called) which was often given, is that we have an *intuitive knowledge* of axioms and basic forms of inference. Nobody has succeeded in explaining just what this means, but perhaps it is connected with the idea that, when we come to consider an example, we can somehow *see*, not only that two right lines meet in at most one point, but also that this must be so. Absolute knowledge is always connected ultimately with visual sensation.[5] The example of Euclidean geometry was, of course, an unfortunate one, but we need not bother with that. Other so-called explanations of the basic mathematical and logical truths are that they are 'self-evident', 'given', or known by a process of 'intuitive induction', or that we can see they are true because 'the contrary implies a contradiction'. None of these phrases means much, and we can count that as further evidence that the problem was not taken seriously.

There was, however, one important feature which all our philosophers believed mathematical and logical truths to possess, and which was promoted by some to the status of a definition. It was supposed that the contradictory of such a truth was unimaginable.[6] In the ordinary sense of 'unimaginable' of course, this could hardly be a sufficient condition for logical truth, although it might be a necessary condition. And if it is a necessary condition, it becomes rather hard to see how one can make mistakes in logic at all, for a mistake consists in believing something false, and how can one believe what one cannot even imagine? This, then, was the situation. It was thought that mathematical knowledge was superior to our ordinary knowledge of matters of fact, and this superiority was connected with the method used to establish the propositions of mathematics. It was supposed that the axiomatic method was somehow *self-guaranteeing*, that is to say, it could be used to prove its own consistency. And finally, it was supposed that the axioms which provide the essential starting point are known by a peculiar and incorrigible process, which can only be described as direct intellectual vision. But no proposition whose contradictory is imaginable can be the object of such direct vision.

Matters of fact are here sharply distinguished from matters of logic and mathematics, but the former field itself admits of some division. Our knowledge of facts may be inferior to our knowledge of mathematics, but no one is ever seriously worried concerning his knowledge of what is going on here and now. Mistakes are possible, but the possibility is exceedingly remote. Of course, philosophers have said we cannot ever know what is going on under our noses (as opposed to sometimes not knowing), but nobody takes them seriously. The same applies to that knowledge of the past allowed us by memory. But when it comes to what is going on in some remote place, or what will happen in the future, we are often impressed by the extent of our ignorance. And often enough we are only too well aware that there is absolutely nothing we can do about it. This profound and quite insoluble conflict between our desire to know what will happen, and our awareness that we cannot know, is one of the real starting points of philosophy.

We are now in a position to assess rather roughly the impact of the new experimental method on the philosophy of the seventeenth century. For the first time in human history a large number of more or less concealed regularities in the course of nature had been brought to light. No doubt the perception of a hidden order in what seems at first sight disordered affords great pleasure and satisfaction to the mind of the discoverer, but to the outsider the most striking thing will always be the utility of such discoveries. Observed regularities can be used very successfully to predict the future, and they can be used to gain power over nature. In this sense, the scientist is the successor of the prophet and the magician: he occupies the place in society formerly held jointly by those two. Now the old prophets claimed a special kind of knowledge of the future, and of what was happening in distant places, something far superior to the natural expectations and beliefs that anyone may form. They claimed to know the future, just as you or I know what is going on directly before our eyes. They claimed direct vision of the future, and of remote events. And the magician claimed the power to *bind* things to act according to his will. Here we can see already the beginning of a conflict, a conflict which soon became acute when the scientist combined both jobs.

Now the obvious thing about the scientist is not that he has prophetic knowledge and magical power in the proper sense of these phrases. The obvious thing about him is that he carries out the functions of prophet and magician with resounding success: he has squeezed everyone else out of the business. His prophecies are frequently fulfilled, and the complex rituals he prescribes usually terminate in the desired result. Why is the scientist successful? This is the question which occupied the attention of philosophers, and it was natural to suppose that the answer lay in the fact that the scientist really did have the key to the prophetic knowledge and magical power which his predecessors falsely claimed to possess. And we have already seen that pure mathematics had become the model of absolute or perfect knowledge. Consequently, justifications of science took the form of attempts to connect the empirical method of physical science with the axiomatic method of pure mathematics.

The resulting theories fell roughly into two classes. First, we have theories in which the experimental method is considered only as an initial step in the direction of perfect knowledge of the physical world. Second, we have theories in which the experimental method is itself regarded as supplying such knowledge. In the first kind of theory, it was supposed that the elucidation of concealed regularities in the course of natural events must be supplemented by a further discipline, variously defined. The result of a successful pursuit of this further discipline was believed to be the acquisition of an intuitive insight into certain fundamental principles of nature. These principles resembled the axioms of geometry in two respects; they were to be known in the same sort of way, that is by an incorrigible intuition; and they were to serve as starting points for deductive inference. The only differences between the philosopher's principles and the axioms of geometry lay in the manner by which the appropriate intuition was to be acquired, and, what is more important, in the nature of what was to be deduced. For it was supposed that facts about the past and future could be deduced from these intuitively known principles. And then the philosopher's knowledge of the future would share the peculiar immunity of mathematical knowledge.

The other kind of theory was aimed more directly at the

DAVID HUME

same objective. Here intuitive knowledge of fundamental
principles of nature was restricted to certain principles of a
very general character, which later acquired the names of
'Law of Universal Causation' and 'Law of the Uniformity
of Nature'. It was not supposed that the course of future
events could be deduced from these principles alone, but it
was supposed that they served, so to speak, to connect the
past and present with the future. That is to say, it was believed
that such principles would enable us to deduce future events
from our knowledge of past and present events. For example,
the law of Uniformity of Nature says that past regularities
will continue in the future, and a particular example of this
is that, if heat has always resulted in boiling water, then it
will continue to do so. From this conditional alone, we can
deduce nothing whatever about the actual course of events;
but if we know also that heat always has resulted in boiling
water, then we may deduce that it will always do so. Thus,
knowledge of the uniformity of nature will provide us with
knowledge of the future which is at least as good as our
knowledge of the present and of the past.

These, then, are our two kinds of theory about scientific
knowledge. In the first theory, the aim of scientific investigation is ultimately to acquire intuitive knowledge of certain
axioms, from which all (and only) true statements of fact may
be deduced, whether past, present, or future. In the second
theory, the aim of scientific investigation is first to discover
regularities, and then to obtain axioms which will logically
guarantee the permanence of these regularities, so that we
may deduce the future from the past. Whatever the merits of
the latter theory may be, it is clear that the appropriate law
of uniformity will require very careful statement, for it is
quite clear to us that not all observed regularities are in fact
permanent. Thus, we need a way of sorting observed regularities into those which are permanent, and those which are
not. Suppose A has always been succeeded by B, how are we
to decide whether this is a permanent regularity or not? The
answer usually given really amounts to quite a different
theory. It is that we can tell that the sequence A to B is per-

manent by seeing a *causal connexion* between A and B. If we see this causal connexion, then we see that A must be succeeded by B, and hence that A always will be succeeded by B. But if we admit anything like this, the law of uniformity becomes redundant, because the causal connexion by itself is supposed to guarantee the connexion between A and B.

It cannot be stressed too strongly that Hume's criticism of these theories is really directed at their common root, namely the notion that absolute or perfect knowledge is possible for man. We have already seen that real knowledge was apt to be *contrasted* with naturally formed expectations and beliefs, and it is precisely this contrast that Hume rejects. But this does not appear at once, because his first aim is to show that the empirical sciences cannot be raised to the level of mathematical knowledge. Next he constructs a positive theory of the nature of scientific inquiry, based on his criticism of earlier theories. Last, he tries to show that mathematics itself is suspect, and cannot serve as a model of perfect knowledge.

Hume has left us two accounts of his theory of knowledge, one in the *Treatise of Human Nature*, and another in the *Enquiry concerning Human Understanding*. A convenient starting point is the first two paragraphs in Section IV of the *Enquiry*. Here he says that all the objects of human enquiry may be divided into two kinds, Relations of Ideas and Matters of Fact.[7] Relations of Ideas include geometry, algebra, and arithmetic, and 'every affirmation which is either intuitively or demonstratively certain'. Their chief characteristic is that they are 'discoverable by the mere operation of thought alone, without dependence on what is anywhere existent in the universe'. The negation of such truths 'implies a contradiction', and so 'cannot be distinctly conceived by the mind'. Matters of Fact are not 'intuitively or demonstratively certain', the negation of any truth of fact does not imply a contradiction, and can be distinctly conceived by the mind. We may assume, although Hume does not actually say so, that statements of fact depend for their truth on what is existent somewhere in the universe.

We must pause for a moment to notice that Hume gives here what seems to be two different methods of classifying

'the objects of human enquiry', namely the method of truth
conditions, and the method of verification processes. Statements of fact depend for their truth on what exists in the universe, whereas statements about relations between ideas do
not. And statements about relations between ideas are verified by intuition and deduction, whereas statements of fact
are not. It is not obvious that these two methods of classification will yield the same result, although Hume clearly as-
sumes that this is so. The assumption is simply that no existential statements are provable (in the mathematical sense).
This is important, because it entails immediate rejection of
all theories of the first type mentioned above, for these claim
that all true statements are provable, and hence of course
that all true existential statements are provable. The only
way of escape is to say there are no existential statements,
that is, no statements which depend for their truth on what
actually exists in the universe, and this involves saying that
truth does not consist in correspondence with reality, a step
which was actually taken by some philosophers.[8] Thus, there
are two things Hume takes for granted: (1) If a statement is
provable, then its negation cannot be clearly conceived, and
(2) The negation of every statement of fact can be clearly
conceived. It follows at once that no statement of fact is
provable. It remains to consider whether, given some statement of fact A, we can use it to prove some other statement of
fact B. Evidently this is possible only in those cases where the
truth of A is incompatible with the falsity of B, and by our
assumption, this means that the joint truth of A and falsity of
B must be inconceivable. It is obvious that if A says something about the present (or the past), and B says something
about the future, the joint truth of A and falsity of B is never
inconceivable; and so statements about the present and the
past can never be used to prove statements about the future.
Consequently, we cannot use our knowledge of the present
and the past to acquire knowledge of the future, or if we do,
the method used cannot be the method of proof. This is the
substance of Hume's criticism.

It is worth looking at Hume's detailed treatment of this

point, because it has an important bearing on his own theory. He says that, from the fact that bread has nourished us in the past, we conclude that the bread we now eat will nourish us in the future. By bread we mean something that has been manufactured in a certain way from certain ingredients, and nothing more. It is quite clear that we cannot deduce from the fact that this is bread, that it will nourish us; for if this were so we could know that bread would nourish us, even before we had eaten any, and we do not know any such thing. It is only by experience that we find out what is nourishing and what is not. On the other hand, it does not follow from the fact that bread has nourished us in the past, that it will continue to do so. The contrary may, as Hume says, be clearly conceived. We can always imagine a change in the laws of nature, and so, on Hume's assumptions, the impossibility of any such change can never be proved. Now, as pointed out previously, philosophers have tried to avoid this conclusion by introducing a general premiss to the effect that observed regularities continue. It is true that the fact that bread always has nourished us, together with this principle of the continuation of observed regularities, suffice to prove that bread will continue to nourish us. But the whole weight of the problem is then transferred to this principle. It is not provable, and is in fact false.

The other theory that Hume attacks is rather more complicated. It is more complicated because originally it was quite a different sort of theory, and its purpose was to answer a different question. We can ask how we know bread will nourish us, and we can ask why bread will nourish us. Theories about how we know are epistemological theories, and these form our present business. Theories about reasons why might be called explanatory theories, and they occupied a prominent position in ancient philosophy. For reasons which I have tried to make clear, philosophers of Hume's period were preoccupied with epistemological problems, and explanatory problems tended to fall into the background. There was, however, one theory of very early origin which had a strong hold over many minds. This was the theory that things behaved in the way they did in virtue of possession of certain causal powers or properties.[9] These powers were conceived somewhat naïvely as residing in objects, or rather they were conceived as being just like the other qualities of objects, except that they were hidden from view. For example, it might be supposed that bread nourishes in virtue of possessing a power of nourishment, and this power is regarded as a quality of bread, just as whiteness and softness are qualities of bread. The only difference is that, whereas whiteness and softness of bread are immediately apparent to the beholder, the power of nourishment is hidden from view. Then if we could bring this hidden power or quality to light, we should be in a position to know that bread is nourishing, in just the same way as we know that it is white and soft, namely by direct perception. This notion of hidden or occult powers and qualities had been the object of hostile comment, even in the seventeenth century, and by Hume's time it was largely abandoned by empirical scientists. For example, when Newton announced that he proposed no hypotheses, he did not of course mean that he made no generalizations from experience, for his work consisted wholly of such generalizations.[10] What he meant was that he proposed no *explanatory* hypotheses, and by that he meant to avoid talking about hidden powers in bodies whose presence would explain the phenomena of gravitation and so forth.

Now, although this doctrine of hidden powers and occult qualities had been abandoned by practical scientists, it remained interesting and attractive to those philosophers who wished to preserve for mankind the possibility of a kind of perfect knowledge of the future. For, in order to know that this bread will nourish us if eaten, we need only ascertain that it possesses the hidden power of nourishing us. So if we could come to see this power in the same way as we see the whiteness of bread, we should see that it will nourish us. We should, so to speak, be in a position to see the future in the present, and to know the future with as much certainty as we know the present. So, at least, it would appear to the uncritical mind. Hume produces several arguments against this view.

68

His first point is that these powers in things, if they exist at all, are in fact hidden from us at first.[11] Nitrates, for example, presumably have the power to cause growth in plants, but no examination of nitrates alone will tell us this. The only test which tells us that nitrates encourage growth and chlorides do not, is the addition of nitrates to the soil in one case, and chlorides in another, and leaving the soil in its natural state in a third. Then we observe that the plants with nitrates do better than the others. If there is a way of knowing that nitrates have the power of encouraging growth in plants, this is the only way. Furthermore, one test taken alone will not establish the fact: you need many such tests before drawing any conclusion.

The people who believe in occult qualities would agree with all this. Their theory is that the power of nitrates is hidden at first, and gradually emerges into view in the course of the experiments. That is to say, after doing the experiments you come to see something new that you did not see before, namely the power of the nitrates. You actually see something about nitrates that you did not see before, not metaphorically but really. Once having come to see this power, you are in a position to know the future, to see the future in the present. This is the theory which attempts to square the experimental acquisition of knowledge with the doctrine of the perfectibility of knowledge. Experiment reveals the hidden power, and seeing the power enables you to deduce the future from the present. This is one theory of scientific inference: that the laws of nature, or rather the powers in things which explain and guarantee the continued operation of those laws, really are discovered, in the sense of being exposed to view.

It is quite obvious that this account of how we learn from experience is constructed so as to ensure that the knowledge gained by experience is the best possible kind of knowledge. Hume's objection is simply that it is a false account.[12] Suppose we consider the statement that salt is soluble in water. It is agreed that we can know this only by experience. But what exactly is the experience? We see the salt immersed in water, and then we see it dissolve. We do not see anything about the salt that necessitates its dissolving: all we see is that it does in fact dissolve. And even if we perform the experiment a large number of times, we never see anything more. We never see in addition the power that makes the salt dissolve.

This argument is an example of the application of what Hume calls his 'experimental method of reasoning', and it is worth pausing for a moment to see just what it amounts to. All he really says here is that his opponents claim we sometimes see something which we never do in fact see. And he proposes to establish this by inviting us to consider attentively what we do see in such cases, and to ask ourselves whether we see anything we should describe as a power. He is quite confident that our answer will be that we do not. As an argument it is persuasive rather than conclusive. We shall return to this point later on.

In the meantime it is important to notice that Hume used another kind of argument, which is to my mind perfectly conclusive. This is the argument that even if the doctrine of hidden powers were true, it would not do the work required of it, and is therefore redundant.[13] For suppose you could somehow see that this lump of salt had the power of dissolving in water. Then all that this would show you is that if it were now in water, it would be dissolving – a useless, if interesting, item of information. But possession of the power now could not guarantee that in future it will dissolve, because this event does not depend on present possession of the power, but on its future possession. And if a thing can have a power, it can lose it too. Consequently, even if you could see that salt had the power of dissolving in water, you could not deduce from this that it will dissolve when it is put in water at some future time. I have pointed out before that the doctrine of hidden powers was not invented in order to show that knowledge of the future is possible: it was invented in order to provide explanations of why things behave as they do. But it was invoked by some people to show that such knowledge is possible. Hume's point is that it is invoked in vain.

To sum up so far: (1) Hume shows, conclusively to my mind, that certain theories designed to show how we can

deduce the future from the past are fallacious. (2) He also
shows that in ordinary life we never do in fact deduce the
future from the past. His argument here is that, if we did,
we should know how it was done, and philosophers would
not be driven to constructing false theories about it.[14] (3) He
does *not* show conclusively that it is impossible ever to deduce
the future from the past.[15] (4) He is, however, convinced that
it *is* impossible, as are all philosophers of his temper, and his
examination of the question is designed primarily to persuade
us to accept this conclusion.

We may now turn to Hume's own positive theory of scientific inference. It is absolutely essential here to understand
that his theory is quite different in kind from those we have
been discussing. The purpose of those theories was either to
justify scientific method as it stands, or to exhibit a new im-
proved method which is justified. And a justified method was
conceived as one which, if properly used, could not ever lead
to false propositions. The initial question is: What ought we
to believe? And the answer to this is, of course, that we ought
to believe only what is true. Then we ask how we are to distinguish true propositions from false ones, so that we may
repose our belief only in the former. In the case of a proposition which asserts something about what is happening here
and now, we have only to look and see if it is true. But if a
proposition asserts something about what is happening in a
distant place, or what will happen in the future, we cannot
just look and see: we must either go and see, or wait and see.
Now the question is raised: How can we decide what will
happen in the future, without waiting to see? And the answer
given was that propositions about the future are true if they
have been arrived at by a certain method. The whole difficulty was to define this method satisfactorily: for it will have
to be a method which can be guaranteed to give the same
results here and now as we should get if we cared to wait and
see. Hume maintains, rightly in my opinion, that there is no
such method. This is why his own theory is different in kind
from those we have just discussed.

We see now that the whole programme of these philosophers

rests on the questions: What ought we to believe? and: What method ought we to adopt to secure that our beliefs shall be true? These questions presuppose that our beliefs are a matter of choice. They assume that we are capable of surveying various possibilities, and of choosing which to believe and which not to believe. Thus Descartes supposed he could doubt everything except his own existence.[16] Hume's position is the antithesis of this. He does not actually say we have no choice about what we shall believe, but it is quite clear that he thinks our powers of choice in this connexion are very much more restricted than philosophers like Descartes had supposed. And he is quite right. Once we have been burned by fire, we believe that fire will burn us again if we touch it. It is not a matter of choice: it is more than we can do not to believe. The belief that fire will burn is a natural reaction to having been burned, just as anger is a natural reaction to insult. There is no process of rational inference involved at all. Hume sums up his position in the following words.[17]

Belief is the necessary result of placing the mind in such circumstances. It is an operation of the soul, when we are so situated, as unavoidable as to feel the passion of love, when we receive benefits; or hatred, when we meet with injuries. All these operations are a species of natural instincts, which no reasoning or process of thought and understanding is able either to produce or to prevent.

It is easy to see that this constitutes a total rejection of the assumption upon which the rationalist programme was ultimately based. There can therefore be no question of what method we ought ideally to use in order to arrive at beliefs. All that can be accomplished is an account of how in fact beliefs do arise in the human mind. This is the task that Hume sets himself.

II

Hume tries to answer two questions, which he puts in these words:

(1) Why we conclude that such particular causes must necessarily have such particular effects, and why we form an inference from one to the other.

72

(2) What is our idea of necessity, when we say that two objects are necessarily connected together?

He has ruled out the following two questions:

(3) Does the manner in which we arrive at conclusions concerning causes and effects, guarantee in any way the truth of those conclusions?
(4) What method ought we to adopt in order to secure that we should arrive only at true conclusions?

That is to say, he believes there can be no question of justification, but only of description and analysis. The first question will be answered in the terminology of impressions and ideas; and will utilize the theories of association of ideas, and of the generation of beliefs. The second question is more difficult, and requires some preliminary explanation.

Hume takes it for granted that two things are essential, but not sufficient, for causal connexion, namely the effect must immediately succeed the cause, and the effect must be spatially contiguous to the cause.[19] He calls these two features the *conjunction* of cause and effect. His explanation of how we come to infer an effect B from a cause A, is that we have observed A and B constantly conjoined in the past, and so the ideas of A and B become associated, according to the principles explained under association of ideas. Then, if we see A, the idea of B occurs to us, and is raised to the status of a belief in virtue of its association with the impression A. In other words, if we always see A followed by B, we get into the habit of expecting B when we see A. It is evident that this describes a common occurrence, no matter what objections there may be to Hume's terminology of impressions and ideas. When we see A always followed by B, we often do get into the habit of expecting B, and moreover the formation of this habit is often independent of rational choice. Thus, according to Hume, causal inference is nothing more than customary expectation.[20] It is not inference at all in the strictly rational sense.

So far, Hume has explained, with some show of plausibility, how we come to 'form an inference' from A to B, that is, how we come to expect B whenever A occurs. But he has not explained how we come to believe, or to say, that A *causes* B, or that B is a *necessary result* of A. The natural consequence of his account is either that, when we say A causes B, we mean only that A and B have always occured in conjunction; or we mean that we have formed a habit of expecting B whenever A occurs. The first alternative does not seem strong enough, and the second seems absurd. For on the second alternative, A causes B only when we have formed a certain habit, and not before. Thus the objection is that Hume's account of causal inference, taken in its simplest form, gives an inadequate, or an absurd meaning to the words 'cause' and 'necessity'. It is for this reason that it is essential for him to answer the second of his two questions: What is our idea of necessity? He must try to give an analysis of necessity which will agree with his account of causal inference, and which will at the same time retain intuitive plausibility.

Hume's method of analysis is to consider the idea for which words like 'cause' and 'necessity' stand. And this means discovering the impression from which the idea is derived. Now Hume has been at some pains to prove that we never do have an impression of causal connexion. Consequently, we never have an idea of causal connexion, and the word 'cause' must be meaningless. It thus seems impossible that Hume should attempt a positive account of the nature of causality, as distinct from an account of how we come to form expectations. And yet he does make such an attempt: he simply cannot bring himself to say that the word 'cause' is meaningless. He wants to say it cannot mean what we think it means, and so must really mean something other than we think. There is evidently some kind of confusion here, the source of which we must try to locate.

Hume gives two definitions of 'cause', as follows: [21]

[A cause is] an object precedent and contiguous to another, and where all the objects resembling the former are placed in a like relation of precedency and contiguity to those objects that resemble the latter.

74

A cause is an object precedent and contiguous to another, and so united with it, that the idea of the one determines the mind to form the idea of the other, and the impression of the one to form a more lively idea of the other.

He says that the first defines 'cause' considered as a philosophical relation, and the second defines 'cause' considered as a natural relation. The import of the first definition is clear enough: it simply states that causal connexion (as a philosophical relation) is nothing over and above uniformity of sequence. There is only one doubtful point: we are not quite sure whether Hume means only that A always has preceded B, or both that A always has preceded B, and always will precede B. We may take the latter interpretation as more plausible, at least for the present. Evidently we have here a perfectly reasonable definition of causal connexion. It is not invalidated by Hume's destructive analysis, because the object of that analysis is not to show that we have no idea of uniformity of sequence, but rather to show that we have no idea of anything which *compels* or *enforces* such uniformity. He might well have rested content with this definition, which is a natural, and indeed an inevitable outcome of his method of philosophy. The meaning and purpose of the second definition (of cause as a natural relation) is much more obscure. It is hard to understand what led Hume to produce this second definition, and how it is related to the first.

One way of understanding a puzzling statement in philosophy is to consider the use made of it by the philosopher in question. The chief use of Hume's second definition of causality is to explain why the first definition seems inadequate. Or, rather, that is how he tries to use it: the question of his success is another matter. The point is that Hume is not content to say that causality is nothing more than uniformity of sequence: he wants to explain how people mistakenly came to suppose that it was something more, namely something that enforced uniformity. How did they come to think that causality, as a necessary connexion, is something more than uniformity of sequence? He has to explain this in face of the fact that he has proved we cannot even have any idea of

75

necessary connexion, at least between objects in the external world. How can people mistakenly suppose that a word means something they cannot even conceive? This is the problem that ultimately faces all philosophical reductionists, or users of the phrase 'nothing but'. It is to Hume's credit that he faced up to it, even if he did not solve it.

We have already noted that Hume has a general method for solving problems of this kind, and this method is based on two principles. The first is that, if two ideas are closely associated in some way, we are apt to mistake one for the other. The second is that, if some object arouses a certain feeling in our minds, we are apt to project that feeling on to the object, and to regard it as a real quality of the object.[22] Only the latter of these two principles is utilized in the present case. In brief, Hume says that, just as we speak of a sad scene, although the sadness is really in the spectator, so do we speak of forces compelling uniformity in the external world, although these forces are really in the mind of the spectator. To understand what this means, we need first a clear and convincing instance of the general principle, and second a more detailed account of its application.

A clear case of projection occurred during the late war, when people wrote to the newspapers complaining of the gloomy and despondent note put forth by air-raid sirens. Why, they asked, could not the authorities have arranged for these to play some cheerful and encouraging tune, like 'Britannia Rules the Waves'? The answer was, of course, that the note of the sirens was not despondent or alarming, but its acquired associations induced despondency in the hearer. Even if they had played 'Britannia Rules the Waves', people would soon have complained of a hitherto unsuspected menace in that tune. The projection was in fact nearly complete for most people: the warning note was actually felt as menacing, and the note at the end of a raid really sounded cheerful. But it could have been the other way round, and so we are intellectually convinced that the warning note was not in itself menacing, although it became impossible to imagine or to feel it as otherwise. This example brings out two important points. The first is that the siren note did not in itself induce alarm, but only through its associations which were the product of experience. Nevertheless, it did come to sound alarming in itself. The second point is that, even when we are intellectually convinced that the sound is not in itself alarming, nonetheless we cannot, so to speak, feel or envisage it as cheerful, or neutral in effect.

Hume's use of the principle of projection in the case of causation, is not quite parallel with our example, but it is close enough. It will be remembered that, in his account of causal inference, he says that, if we have two objects or events A and B, the idea of A is not at first associated with the idea of B, and experience of A does not produce expectation of B. Then, after some experience of constant conjunction, the idea of A becomes associated with the idea of B, and experience of A does produce expectation of B. He now expresses himself more strongly. He says that, after experience of constant conjunction, it is not merely the case that experience of A is *always followed* by expectation of B, but also that, on experiencing A, *we feel compelled* to expect B.[23] It is not simply that the expectation always follows, or even that we *are* compelled, but we have a *feeling* of compulsion. It is this feeling of compulsion, that we have to expect B on the occurrence of A, which is projected to to the events themselves, and is as it were seen as a compulsion on A to produce B. The sense of compulsion in us appears as a necessary relation between external objects, just as the despondency in us appears as an intrinsic quality of the siren's warning note. And just as our intellectual conviction that sounds cannot be despondent has no influence on how we feel, so our intellectual conviction that causal power cannot reside in objects cannot influence our feeling that it does so reside. The parallel is quite close. We say a sound is melancholy, and someone objects: 'How can a sound be melancholy? Surely only conscious beings can be melancholy, what you must mean is that the sound makes you, or most people, melancholy. How could you possibly detect melancholy in a *sound?*' Then we say A causes B, or A compels B, and Hume objects: 'How can you

77

see or feel B being compelled by A? You cannot feel something else being compelled, but *you can feel compelled*. So when
you say A causes B, what you must mean is that the occurrence of A compels you to expect B.'

Some account of Hume's theory of belief has now been given,
and we have seen that it is an account of how beliefs do in
fact arise in the human mind. He does not undertake to tell
us how we ought to proceed, but how we do proceed, how in
fact as human beings we are bound to proceed. There is
throughout an implicit suggestion that belief is not an object
of choice. It is this aspect of his theory, rather than its psychological correctness, which is of prime epistemological importance. It remains to consider in more detail how Hume's
theory bears on the epistemological problem, and on the
ancient doctrine of Scepticism.

Scepticism may be total or partial, in the following sense:
the total sceptic says that nothing can be known, the partial
sceptic says only that matters of fact cannot be known. We
shall see that Hume reveals himself as a total sceptic, although
he often appears disguised as a partial sceptic. But before examining his arguments for total scepticism, we must try to
clear up a few possible misconceptions. First and foremost, a
sceptic says that we cannot *know* anything, he does not say
that we cannot feel certain about anything, and he does not
say that all, or even most of the things about which we feel
certain are false. The doctrine of scepticism is perfectly consistent with the statement that on most occasions when we
feel certain we are right, and it is probably consistent with
the statement that whenever we feel certain we are right.
That is to say, if scepticism can be maintained at all, it could
probably be maintained even though all the beliefs anyone
held were always true. I say this is probable, and not certain,
only because one of the arguments in favour of scepticism
rests on the assumption that people do sometimes entertain
false beliefs. Apart from this, it should be obvious that the
sceptic can only claim that nothing can be known: he cannot

consistently claim to *know* that nothing can be known. Consequently the arguments he produces will be attempts to secure conviction rather than to impart knowledge of the truth of his doctrine.

We have already seen that the arguments for partial scepticism, or scepticism concerning matters of fact, depend for their force on the difference between the way in which we acquire beliefs about relations between ideas (as expressed in the propositions of logic and mathematics), and the way in which we acquire beliefs about matters of fact. It is supposed that the former are acquired by direct intuition, and by deductive inference; whereas the latter are acquired by sensory perception, and by causal inference. The other assumption is that a belief amounts to knowledge if and only if it is acquired by direct intuition, or by valid deductive inference from what is already known. If we ignore certain minor points, attempts to show that matters of fact can be known, or could be known, are transformed into attempts to show that causal inference either is, or could be replaced by, deductive inference. Hume shows that these latter alternatives are alike impossible, and hence that we cannot know any matters of fact. We now see that this argument for scepticism rests on a certain assumption about knowledge, namely that a belief amounts to knowledge if and only if it is acquired by direct intuition, or by valid deductive inference from what is already known. That is to say, a belief is knowledge if and only if it has a certain kind of history, what we might call a logical history.

It is obviously important in the study of scepticism, and in epistemology generally, to ask what grounds there are for this assumption. Why should beliefs with a sound logical history, and these alone, rank as knowledge? One way of circumventing this question is to say it is not an assumption at all, but a definition of knowledge. Much of what Hume and other empiricists say suggests that, at least at times, they regard the matter in this light. But this is little more than a piece of prevarication: its only merit is to raise another question, which does perhaps make the situation a little clearer.

The point is that if a belief is to rank as knowledge, it must be a *true* belief. This is a necessary, if not a sufficient condition. Consequently, if you define knowledge as beliefs with a logical history, you must be assuming that all beliefs with a logical history are true beliefs. Now I think the assumption actually made is something stronger than this. I think it is assumed that the statement: 'If a belief has a logical history, it is true', is itself a logical truth, and itself has, or could be provided with, a logical history. Perhaps it is supposed to be self-evident: the reader may well ponder the matter. The meaning of this kind of scepticism is now plain. The sceptic says we may know matters of logic, but not matters of fact. By this he means matter of logic can have a logical history, and beliefs of fact cannot. He then implies that, since only a logical history guarantees the truth of a belief, beliefs of fact may always be false, no matter how they are acquired. That is what he really means when he says no matter of fact can be known. If his argument is valid at all, it is valid even if all the factual beliefs actually held by anybody are always true.

The argument for total scepticism is of a different character, and perhaps it even establishes a different sort of scepticism. It depends essentially on the actual occurrence of false beliefs, and it is expounded by Hume in the *Treatise*, Book 1, Part 4. The argument is closely connected with Hume's theory of probability, which we must first consider. In this connexion, it must be clearly understood that, according to Hume's principles, there can be no question of discovering some method for assigning probabilities, which is logically certain to give correct results. Such a method demands *a priori* knowledge of a principle of uniformity, the possibility of which Hume has already denied in his treatment of causal inference. The only problem that remains is how we come to feel perfectly certain about some of our conclusions, and more or less uncertain about others. Hume's answer is, roughly speaking, that we feel perfectly confident that B will follow A on this present occasion, if it has always done so on past occasions, and if the present occasion exactly resembles the past occasions. We feel fairly confident, if B has followed

A more often than not, or if the present occasion closely resembles the past occasion; and so on. Our confidence adjusts itself in this manner. He gives a complicated account of the mental processes whereby he supposes this adjustment to take place, but we need not consider these. The important point is that assessments of probability are not, and cannot be, arrived at by rational means (that is, by deduction from intuitively self-evident principles).

Now we may observe that, even in the deductive sciences of logic and mathematics, we do in fact sometimes make mistakes. The exact nature of these mistakes is something of a puzzle, if we take seriously the doctrine that we cannot even conceive what is logically false. But when we make a mistake, in, for example, an arithmetical sum, the result of our mistake is certainly a *belief* in something that is logically false. The result of this observation is to destroy the privileged character of our judgements in mathematics and logic. We have noticed that this privilege consisted in the fact that if propositions of logic have a certain kind of history, or are arrived at by a certain kind of ritual, namely intuition and logical deduction, they must necessarily be true. For statements of fact, on the other hand, there is no history or ritual which they can have, and which will guarantee their truth in this manner. This is the difference we have in mind when we say that matters of logic are knowable, and matters of fact are not knowable. It is now suggested by the sceptic that, in order to know a matter of logic, it is necessary, *but not sufficient*, that it should be arrived at by correct performance of the logical ritual. The sceptic says we must also *know* that it was acquired in this way. The occurrence of errors in logic indicates that our confidence that the ritual was correctly performed does not in any way guarantee that it was in fact correctly performed. Moreover, although a matter of logic is a matter of logic, the fact that it was correctly deduced is not a matter of logic: it is a matter of fact. Consequently, we cannot know any matter of logic, unless we already know a matter of fact, to wit the fact that it was correctly deduced. Since it has already been established that we cannot know any matter of fact whatever (although, of course, we may be convinced of it, and it may be true), it follows that we cannot ever know any matter of logic. The reader should note that this argument depends essentially on the assumption that knowledge of a matter of logic demands, not only that it should be arrived at by correct intuition and deduction, but also that we should know that this is the case. Assumptions of this character are often imported into philosophical arguments without acknowledgement. They may or may not be justified.

The argument just given does not really depend on the actual occurrence of error, but only on the factual character of our belief that deduction has been correctly performed. It would hold, even if we never made any mistakes. But it is argued by Hume that, because we do make mistakes, no belief in the correct performance of our deductions can be more than probable. For example, we feel certain that some particular deduction is correct. We know from experience that sometimes we have felt certain a deduction is correct, and then afterwards found it was not. Therefore it is only probable that this present deduction is correct. Surely, then, we should modify our assurance. Surely, on these grounds, we are never justified in feeling certain about any deduction. Even the simplest deductions are dubious, because a complex deduction is made up of a number of simple steps, and if there is a mistake in a complex deduction, it must be in one or more of the simple steps. You will notice that a question of justification is raised here: 'we are never justified in feeling certain'. We ought to doubt even that twice two is four.

Hume next proceeds to an even stranger argument, and one which, in my opinion, is of little value. It runs approximately as follows.[24] Suppose we find by experience that we make mistakes half the time. Then, when we are sure of anything, we ought to assign to it probability $1/2$. One of the things we are sure of is that we make mistakes half the time. So this has probability $1/2$. Then Hume *appears* to argue that, if we are sure of the occurrence of some event X, we should conclude that X has a probability of $1/2$. Then we are no

82

longer sure of X, but we are sure that X has probability 1/2, and since everything we are sure of has probability 1/2, the fact that X has probability 1/2, *itself* has probability 1/2. Hume then appears to proceed in somewhat the following fashion: since the fact that X has probability 1/2 itself has probability 1/2, X must really have probability 1/4 (or at any rate, some probability less than 1/2); and this is made the first step in an infinite regress, by means of which we can show that the probability of X must be less than any positive value we care to assign. In the limit, the probability of the occurrence of X must be zero, and so also must be the probability of the non-occurrence of X, by parity of reasoning. If this argument were correct, it would show that we cannot consistently assign any finite probability to any event whatever. Furthermore, if we assume that the strength of our belief in the occurrence of an event should be proportioned to some prior assignment of probability, we should not consistently repose any degree of belief in the occurrence of anything whatever. Hume concludes that, since in spite of this argument we do continue to believe many things, our beliefs are not, and cannot be, the outcome of any rational calculation of probability. This is the point he really wants to make.

The argument just given is obviously invalid, but any criticism of it must take account of two facts. First, it may not be a true representation of what Hume had in mind. Second, even if it was Hume's argument, the fact that it is invalid does not by itself refute the conclusion he wanted to draw. At most, the argument does not as it stands establish that conclusion, and it remains to be seen if it can be corrected. The point of failure occurs where it is argued that, since the fact that X has probability 1/2 itself has probability 1/2, X must have probability 1/4. It is quite obvious that the assignment of probability 1/2 to the claim that X has probability 1/2, does not entail *any* definite probability for X. Any assumption to the contrary must transgress the principle that the sum of the probabilities of X and of not-X should be unity, as indeed is shown by the nature of Hume's conclusion.

It may be, of course, that this principle cannot be consistently applied; but Hume has not demonstrated this, although he certainly did not apply it in this argument.

The error is so obvious that it casts some doubt on our rendering of Hume at this point. Some further examination is needed, and much here depends on the sense we attach to the word 'probable'. The simplest sense is to agree to say that X has probability m/n under conditions K, if in the past X has occurred on just m out of the n occasions when K has occurred. Understood in this sense, it is plain that the statement that X has probability m/n under conditions K entails nothing whatever about the future. In particular, it does not entail that X will occur on exactly, or even approximately, m of the next n occasions when conditions K are realized. This is really all that Hume needs for his kind of scepticism, but either he does not see this, or else he is now interested in some deeper aspect of the situation. We have to ask ourselves what this might be.

Our next task is to define two distinct concepts of reasonable belief, which I shall call reasonable belief (1), and reasonable belief (2). By reasonable belief (1) we mean a belief whose strength is adjusted to probability, calculated by previous frequency as above explained. Thus, always supposing that we can measure the strength of a belief, a belief of strength m/n in the present occurrence of X will be a reasonable belief (1), if we know that K is occurring, and also that on the *previous* n occasions when K occurred, there were just m occasions when X occurred. A reasonable belief (2), on the other hand, is a belief based on knowledge of the future. A belief of strength m/n in the present occurrence of X will be a reasonable belief (2), if we know that K is occurring, and also that on the *next* n occasions when K occur (including the present occasion), there will be just m occasions when X occurs. We observe that a reasonable belief (1) is a belief adjusted to our knowledge of the past, and a reasonable belief (2) is a belief adjusted to our knowledge of the future. Since the past never entails anything about the future, the basis for a reasonable belief (1) is never a basis for a reasonable belief (2).

Hume naturally holds that there is no such thing as a reasonable belief (2), since there is no knowledge of the future. The puzzling thing is that he seems also to reject reasonable belief (1) on the ground that computation of probability by past frequency not only entails nothing as to the future, but also is subject to some kind of inherent contradiction. Perhaps he just made a mistake.

CHAPTER 5

REASON AND MORALS

I

MEN do not only think, believe, and know: they also have feelings and perform actions. They love and hate, become angry or afraid, they create and destroy. Their actions are sometimes reasonable, sometimes unreasonable, sometimes virtuous, and sometimes vicious. Centuries of speculation on these matters has produced a kind of jungle called Ethics or Moral Philosophy, into which few philosophers have now the temerity to penetrate. At present it is not even clear what purpose is served by philosophical (as distinct from psychological or anthropological) exploration in this field. It was not always so, of course. The early philosophers were quite clear about what they wanted. They wanted a method for attaining perfect moral virtue, just as they wanted a method for attaining perfect knowledge. And these two aims were believed to be identical. Knowledge is virtue: [1] you cannot do what you know to be wrong, and you must necessarily do what you know to be right. Here the distinction between perfect knowledge and ordinary common-sense knowledge is essential, because it is obvious that we often do do things we know in the ordinary sense to be wrong, and we often refrain from doing things we know in the ordinary sense to be right. The assumption underlying this theory is that vicious conduct is always the outcome of uncontrolled passion, and that virtue consists in the control and proper direction of the passions by the reason. We may perhaps go a little further. Many details in individual theories of this type suggest to us that what these philosophers have in mind is not so much control of human feelings as their complete suppression or elimination. Then the virtuous man will be one whose actions are determined by his knowledge of good and evil, as distinct from one whose actions are the outcome of passion and desire.

86

Here the passions, as such, are regarded as the origin of moral turpitude. But this is an extreme view. The more moderate view was that only an excess of passion is morally dangerous: an excess such as we should still call 'unreasonable'. It was supposed that a knowledge of good and evil secured virtuous conduct by correcting and counterbalancing excesses of feeling, the image being that of a horseman who guides and restrains a spirited mount.

Before we can explain Hume's total rejection of this image, and what he sought to put in its place, a little further elaboration and analysis is required. First, we may notice that the concept of divine or perfect knowledge plays an essential part in the theory. For it is this which enables us to say that knowledge of the good is a sufficient condition for morality, while admitting that ordinary so-called knowledge is, alas, by no means a sufficient condition. Thus we may suppose that Hume's rejection of the theory is a consequence of his rejection of the possibility of perfect knowledge. Second, on this theory the path to knowledge and the path of moral improvement are one and the same. Once you have a clear view of your duty, there is no separate conflict of duty with desire. It is plain that, if the theory is rejected, the path to knowledge will become separated from the path of moral improvement, the latter presenting a completely different kind of problem. For if the conflict of duty and desire remains after we know what our duty is, it is hard to see what other knowledge, or in general what other rational considerations would produce a favourable resolution. The common practice of moral persuasion tends to support both views of the situation. For when a man says with regret or complacency that he knows his duty but cannot or will not perform it, we sometimes try to persuade him by presenting the matter in a stronger light, as we say; just as if the fault lay in his feeble perception of what in the ordinary sense we say he knows quite well. The duty is perceived, but dimly: it does not strike him with its full force. We then consider it our business to make him feel the full force of his obligation, and thus persuade him to fulfil it. That is the technique of persuasion which lends support to the idea that the path to moral improvement consists simply in getting a clear knowledge of what is right and good. The other way of persuading people to do their duty, assuming it to be known, is of course the social method of reward and punishment. If in the scales of man's conduct the prospect of some worldly pleasure outweighs the sense of duty, we judiciously apply a counterweight of worldly pain. And that is the kind of persuasion which leads to the idea that knowing your duty is one thing and deciding to do it quite another.

There are two features common to both the theories I have outlined. One is the basic assumption that there is such a thing as knowing one's duty, knowing what is good and right, and so on. More accurately, perhaps, it is the assumption that knowledge of this kind is included in one or other of the usual kinds of knowledge, that is, knowledge of matters of fact, of natural laws, or of logical truths. The other assumption is that knowledge does exert some direct influence on conduct. Hume's contention is that both these assumptions are false.

It is clear that Hume's position cannot possibly be accepted, or even understood, without a good deal of further explanation. For at first sight it seems quite obviously wrong to say we never know what is right, and that knowledge (of whatever kind) can never directly influence conduct. But it is worth noticing that the first point (no such thing as knowledge of what is right, good, and so on) may be made to follow from the second (knowledge has no direct influence on conduct). For it seems correct to say that *considerations* of what is right do have a direct influence on conduct, and so if such considerations ever merited the name of knowledge, they would in fact be knowledge which directly influenced conduct, contrary to Hume's second contention. It follows that this second contention, that knowledge has no direct influence on conduct, is the fundamental one, and it needs careful examination.

Hume's main arguments are to be found in Part 3 of Book 2 of the *Treatise*, under the title 'Of the Influencing Motives of the Will'. We need not bother for the present with that mysterious entity the Will which seems to intrude here, for its peculiar characteristics, if any, play no essential part in the discussion. Hume could equally well have headed his section 'Of the Influencing Motives of Conduct'. He starts by observing that it is usual, both in philosophy and in common life,[2] 'to talk of the combat of passions and reason, to give preference to reason, and to assert that men are only so far virtuous as they conform themselves to its dictates'. He then states his purpose in the following terms:

> On this method of thinking the greatest part of moral philosophy, ancient and modern, seems to be founded; nor is there an ampler field, as well for metaphysical arguments, as popular declamations, than this supposed pre-eminence of reason above passion. The eternity, invariableness, and divine origin of the former have been displayed to the best advantage: The blindness, unconstancy, and deceitfulness of the latter have been as strongly insisted on. In order to show the fallacy of all this philosophy, I shall endeavour to prove *first*, that reason alone can never be a motive to any action of the will; and *secondly*, that it can never oppose passion in the direction of the will.

There is one possibility of misunderstanding here, which must first be cleared up. In previous contexts Hume has used the word 'reason' to mean the power we have for obtaining knowledge of relations between ideas, or truths of logic. In this sense, our beliefs concerning causal laws are not products of reason. It is important, therefore, to realize that, in the text now before us, the word reason is used to mean *both* our power of acquiring knowledge about relations between ideas, *and* our power of arriving at beliefs about causal connexions. There is no special significance in this change, but it must be remembered in what follows.

There is no special significance in the change, because Hume makes only one assumption about reason in his proof that it can never be a motive to any action. This is the assumption that reason could be a motive if and only if the knowledge or beliefs which are the products of reason can be motives. He then undertakes to prove that no item of knowledge or belief whatever, no matter what its subject-matter may be, *and no matter how it may have been acquired*, can be a motive for action. Thus his proofs, if they apply at all, apply as much to unreasonable and false beliefs, and to superstitions, as they do to reasonable beliefs and to knowledge. In a word, Hume's contention is that beliefs are not motives.

The considerations he puts forward in support of this conclusion have the form of persuasive examples rather than demonstrative proofs. He observes that a knowledge of arithmetic does not by itself determine anyone to any particular course of action, although it may enable a merchant to pay his just debts, if such is his desire.[3] That is to say, the merchant's motive is his honesty and not his knowledge of arithmetic, for the same knowledge may be employed by another merchant to quite a different end. In the same way, our knowledge that there is an apple on the tree, or that water boils when heated, influences our conduct only in so far as we desire apples or boiling water. Hume concludes from such examples that knowledge or belief, whether of relations between ideas or of matters of fact, is never a motive for action. Since there are, in his view, no other kinds of knowledge or belief, he infers that knowledge and belief, of whatever kind, is never a motive. This directly contradicts those who maintain that knowledge that a certain action is morally right, or that a certain object is morally good, does constitute a motive for the performance of that action or for the bringing into existence of that object.

It seems clear from this sort of argument that Hume is willing to admit that knowledge and belief do influence our conduct. All he has shown so far is that they are not the only influences, and that they are not a special kind of influence, called motives (whatever that may mean). There is also a suggestion, not only that knowledge and beliefs cannot be motives, but also that they cannot conflict with motives in the determination of conduct. Lastly, there is some idea that motives have a fundamental role in conduct, whereas knowledge and belief have only a secondary influence. All these points need careful examination.

By a motive, Hume primarily means a wish or desire for something. And by a wish or desire, he means a feeling of attraction to what gives us pleasure, or of aversion from what gives us pain.[4] Consequently, what he is saying is that belief is not desire, that beliefs cannot conflict with desires, and that desire is the fundamental determinant of conduct. The first of these propositions seems both true and obvious. Belief is one thing, and desire is something quite different. But the other two propositions are still not entirely clear in meaning. Let us consider first the statement that desire is the fundamental determinant of conduct. Now if we cut straight through an exceedingly difficult bit of analysis, we can adopt the following interpretation. What Hume means is that our ends or aims are determined solely by our desires, and that our beliefs have no direct influence on these. The function of belief is limited to indicating the *means* whereby our desires may be satisfied. If we want apples, then our belief that these are sold at a certain shop will, no doubt, lead us to that shop. But if we have no particular desire for apples, then our belief will have no particular effect on our conduct. It seems to follow from this that lack of resolution in conduct may be due to two quite separate causes. It may be due to a conflict of desire, or, granted resolution in this matter, it may be due to uncertainty about proper means. Hume's position is that the latter conflict can be resolved by the acquisition of new knowledge or beliefs, but that the former conflict cannot be resolved in this way.

The example Hume uses to illustrate his theory is the ancient one of master and slave. 'Reason', he says, 'is, and ought always to be, the slave of the passions, and can have no other office but to serve and obey them.' This is, of course, deliberately aimed at rationalist philosophers, who have used the same illustration in precisely the opposite sense. They thought that the passions are, or at any rate ought to be, the slaves of reason. For them, rational conduct was conduct governed by knowledge *as opposed to* conduct governed by feeling. In rational conduct, the ends, as well as the means, were supposed to be determined by reason and knowledge.

Hume suggests that in the final analysis conduct must always be governed by feeling, and so there can be no rational conduct in the sense proposed by rationalist philosophers.For him, rational conduct is conduct whose ends are fixed by feeling, independently of reason; but where the means to those ends are efficiently chosen in the light of knowledge and reason.

Now I have already observed that Hume does not prove his case in any strict manner, and so it is out of place to examine and criticize it as if what he says does claim to be a proof. What he does is to present his opinion in a persuasive manner. For example, he tells us that a merchant uses his knowledge or arithmetic only to achieve an independently determined purpose, namely the proper balancing of his accounts. Then what he suggests is that this is exactly the way in which knowledge always influences conduct: it is always used by its possessor to gain some independently determined end, and never for any other purpose. Now the example does undeniably support the generalization, but it is quite obvious that the generalization cannot be deduced from the example. Nor is it a clear case of scientific or inductive inference, although this is what Hume probably thought it was. What we have here is an argument which, although not valid in any ordinary sense, yet retains some force and produces some conviction. Moreover, it represents a type of reasoning often used by Hume, and indeed by all philosophers. It will therefore be in our interest to enumerate the chief characteristics upon which the force of such reasoning seems to depend.

There are just three such characteristics. First, the example does not simply support the generalization: it also operates as a kind of paradigm or model. For, although the conclusion may be put in general terms, what it really says is that *all other cases are exactly similar to the example given*. Thus, the choice of example plays an essential part in the argument. Another example might have carried us in a very different direction if we had used it as a model, but now we shall be predisposed to analyse it in terms of the model we have adopted. The second feature is that we can readily think of a large number of other cases which do precisely fit the pattern of the example given. The merchant's use of his arithmetical knowledge to attain an independently fixed end, namely the balancing of his books, is a clear case of using knowledge as a means to an end. And it does not need much reflection to see that this sort of thing is a part of everyday life: we all spend a great part of out time using knowledge to serve our purposes. The third feature is that, although we can think of cases which do not obviously fit this pattern, these are comparatively rare. For example, knowledge is sometimes said to be valued for its own sake, and not as a means to an end. Then there is moral and religious knowledge, which does not seem to function simply as a means, but influences our ends and purposes as well. The point is, of course, that although these cases do not obviously fit our pattern of the merchant with his arithmetic, it is not at all plain that they do *not* fit this pattern. And we cannot think of examples which clearly and obviously do not fit. It seems that if we examined and analysed the outstanding cases more carefully, they might be made to fit. These, then, are the things that make this type of argument convincing, and it is fair to say that the character of the argument determines the character of the conclusion. No truth of fact or of logic is established by these means. But we are persuaded to view things from one particular vantage-point.

We need not at present consider the problem of knowledge as an end in itself, except to note that Hume has little difficulty in fitting it into his scheme after some judicious pruning and lopping here and there. The role attributed to religious knowledge will be discussed in the next section, which deals with the nature and function of religion in general. We are left with the problem of moral knowledge: what does it consist of, and what part does it play in our lives? Now Hume will have to say that, if there is such a thing as moral knowledge, its sole use must be to serve as a means to independently determined ends. It can never fix the ends themselves, for these are not fixed by knowledge of any kind, but by feeling and desire. Consequently, if morality is defined as prescribing

93

ends or aims of conduct, there can be no such thing as moral knowledge: it will rather be a matter of moral feeling or sentiment. To say you know that a certain action is morally virtuous is rather like saying you know a certain joke or situation is funny. Virtuous conduct provokes in the normal spectator a pleasurable reaction, called moral approval; just as entertaining conduct provokes in the normal spectator a pleasurable reaction, called amusement. And on this theory, disputes about what is right or wrong will be like disputes about what things are funny, or interesting, or boring. The analogy is interesting and, indeed, salutary: for it leaves us with the impression that moral considerations have no natural superiority over other considerations. Moral feelings are no more than items in the balance-sheet of pleasure and pain.

Hume uses one other important argument to support his position. This argument is of special interest because it is widely accepted at the present day, and because it is mistakenly supposed by many to be a conclusive argument. It is in fact persuasive. It is stated by Hume as follows: [6]

In every system of morality, which I have hitherto met with, I have always remarked, that the author proceeds for some time in the ordinary way of reasoning, and establishes the being of a God, or makes observations concerning human affairs; when of a sudden I am surprised to find, that instead of the usual copulations of propositions, *is*, and *is not*, I meet with no proposition that is not connected with an *ought*, or an *ought not*. This change is imperceptible; but is, however, of the last consequence. For as this *ought*, or *ought not*, expresses some new relation or affirmation, 'tis necessary that it should be observed and explained; and at the same time that a reason should be given, for what seems altogether inconceivable, how this new relation can be a deduction from others, which are entirely different from it.

This passage is hard to follow, because Hume does not give us any further details of the systems he is attacking. All we are told is that they proceed by deducing propositions containing *ought* from propositions which do not contain *ought*. In other words, statements of moral obligation are deduced from statements which are not, at least on the face of it, statements of

94

moral obligation. He then says that deductions of this kind seem to him altogether inconceivable, giving as his reason that *ought* signifies a relation which is not mentioned in the premisses from which the alleged deduction is made. The whole argument is put in very general terms, and we cannot appreciate what point is being made, until we have the answers to three questions. First, we must ask what purpose is served by deducing statements of moral obligation from other statements: why did moralists think it important to do this? Second, what exactly were those other statements? Were they statements of fact, for example? Third, just why does Hume find these deductions so utterly inconceivable? The reason he gives is not very clear or convincing.

An answer to the first question calls for some reflection on the purpose of ethical enquiry in general. A complete solution of this difficult problem in meta-philosophy is not needed, but we have to make one or two rather obvious points. Perhaps one of the beginnings of moral philosophy, if we leave aside the high rationalist aim of absolute moral perfection, is the simple fact that people often disagree about what is right or wrong, and they often get into a muddle, and are unable to make up their minds, one way or the other. Of course, morals is not the only field where people disagree and entertain doubts: the difference is that in other kinds of dispute there is usually a recognized way of settling the issue. For example, if there is some question as to the boiling-point of water, this can be ascertained to the satisfaction of all concerned by a scientific test. We place a thermometer in the water, and heat it to boiling, noting the thermometer reading at that point. If someone disputed the result, not on the ground that the thermometer was inaccurate, or something of that kind, but simply saying that this was not the way to ascertain boiling-points, we should laugh at him. It would seem that he did not understand what a boiling-point was. And in general the case is so with all matters of fact: there is a standard way of settling such disputes, and anyone who questions the method simply does not understand the issues. He must think we are talking about something else.

The situation is very similar with arithmetic. If there is some doubt concerning the answer to a sum, there is a standard procedure for finding out, to wit, the procedure embodied in the rules of arithmetic. If someone seriously disputed our answer, not on the ground that we had made a slip in applying the rules, but on the ground that the commonly accepted rules are wrong, his objection would seem quite absurd. We could never take it seriously, even though in our more philosophical moments we might be at a loss to say exactly why we should not. Thus, in matters of fact and matters of logic or mathematics, we feel that we have standard ways of answering questions, ways that cannot seriously be questioned by practical men, no matter how puzzled philosophers may become concerning their ultimate justification. In such matters the meaning of the question is indissolubly linked with the proper way of answering it. Of course it may sometimes be very difficult, or even impossible, to resolve a question of fact or of logic, but in general the difficulties are practical: we can see the way to the answer, but cannot take it because of physical or intellectual obstacles.

In the field of morals the obstacles seem of a different order. Perhaps if we lived in an isolated society with an ancient and firmly established moral code, moral questions would not seem different from any other; but a wider experience, even of the most superficial kind, suggests to us that different civilizations have different moral codes. They do not have different systems of arithmetic, or different ways of finding out facts. Furthermore, anyone who proposes to prove that the earth is flat, by tinkering with the rules of trigonometry, or who expects to gain a fortune by an individual system of accounting, is rightly condemned as a fool or a crook: but one who proposes a new moral code may equally well be a wise man and a saint. Thus it seems that a moral code, that is a set of rules for answering moral questions, is not at all like the rules of arithmetic. Its validity seems open to question, and so requires some real justification. And at the present time it does seem to many people that there is not, and perhaps cannot be, any absolute moral code, and that moral questions must be decided by other means.

We can now begin to see the purpose of Hume's first remark. 'In every system of morality, which I have hitherto met with,' he says, '. . . of a sudden I am surprised to find, that instead of the usual copulations of propositions, *is*, and *is not*, I meet with no proposition that is not connected with an *ought*, or an *ought not*.' This is exactly what you would expect in a system of morality, for the most obvious way of solving the decision problem for moral statements, is to establish some general connexion between them and some factual or quasi-factual statements, for which we already have a fixed and agreed method of decision. Then the answer to any given moral question can be obtained by finding the answer to the appropriate factual or quasi-factual question. For example, it might be suggested that we ought to perform those, and only those, actions which tend to increase the standard of living in the community. Then, for any particular action X, the question: Ought X to be done? is answered by answering the factual question: Does X tend to increase the standard of living? Or it might be held that we ought to do just those things which are pleasing to God; and then the question: Ought X to be done? is converted into the question: Is X pleasing to God? In this example it is assumed that there is a standard method, such as prayer, or consulting a priest, for finding out what is pleasing to God. I have called the question: Is X pleasing to God? a quasi-factual question, because religious people commonly agree that it can be answered by some kind of empirical investigation, although they often differ about what the right procedure is. Consequently, this solution of the moral decision problem is ambiguous: it might mean, we ought to do what we are inclined to do after prayer and meditation, or, we ought to do as the priest advises, or many other things. But all these alternatives are matters of straight empirical inquiry.

This, then, is the sort of theory Hume wishes to reject. He claims that the linkage required, between moral statements on the one hand, and factual statements on the other, is 'altogether inconceivable'. He does not say that it is impossible, because this would have committed him to a positive proof. He just says that it is not proved and explained by those who invoke it, and that he himself does not see how it is possible. Nevertheless, it is fairly clear that he does think it is impossible, and that the supposition that there is such a linkage involves some profound misconception. We have to ask ourselves, just what the linkage amounts to, and why Hume found it so incredible. Our answer to the latter question must be conjectural, since he does not explain his view in so many words.

In the theories we have described, the appropriate connexion between moral statements and factual statements must be a *logical* connexion, or so it appears. Hume evidently thinks this must be so, for he speaks of *deduction*. Furthermore, if the decisions are to be complete, the deduction must be a two-way affair. For example, if you hold the standard-of-living theory of morals, you say *both* that: X ought to be done, is deducible from: X raises the standard of living, *and* that: X raises the standard of living, is deducible from: X ought to be done. And this means that anyone who says: X raises the standard of living, but it ought not to be done, is contradicting himself, just like someone who says: X is two plus two, but not four, or: X is a tetrahedron, but has not got six edges.

We must first mention two fallacious objections to this theory. They are fallacious because they are based on incorrect notions about the nature of logical truth. The first objection says that if, for any two statements P and Q, each is deducible from the other, then P and Q have the same meaning. Then it is said that, since 'X raises the standard of living' does not mean the same as 'X ought to be done', the one cannot be deducible from the other. Now we may admit that the two latter sentences do not mean the same, but the conclusion is not proved, because the other premiss, that mutually deducible statements must mean the same, is false. For example, 'X has four faces' and 'X has six edges' are mutually deducible, but they do not mean the same. It is not to the point to suggest that perhaps this latter pair do mean the same, because the real object of the argument is to separate pairs of this kind from those which involve 'ought'. We see that the argument presented does not succeed in doing this.

The other objection observes that people have frequently disagreed about what, if anything, entails that X ought to be done. Many statements besides 'X raises the standard of living' have been suggested from time to time as candidates, and none have secured widespread agreement. It is suggested, therefore, that none of these statements can entail 'X ought to be done', on the ground that, if they did, there would be no disputing it. Against this, we may point out that many entailments, now conclusively established, have been objects of dispute and disagreement in the past; and the fact that some cases are still objects of dispute is no reason at all for saying they will not be resolved at some future time. All that really follows is that, if anyone does maintain that 'X raises the standard of living', or something of the kind, entails 'X ought to be done', then it is incumbent on him to prove what be says. We may add, if we wish, that we do not in the least see how he would set about proving such a thing. But that is as far as we can go in criticism, along these lines.

It seems likely that Hume's criticism of attempts to deduce 'ought' from 'is' does not follow either of the two incorrect lines we have considered. His theory of logic is that deducibility is a result of certain relations between ideas, and there is no suggestion that the relation must always be that of identity. It remains for us to conjecture what he really had in mind, and we can do this, if we remember that he thinks we have a sense of morality, very much as we have a sense of humour. But we must first elucidate certain distinctions, and this in turn calls for description of some hypothetical situations.

Let us suppose we are in a foreign country, and are obliged to learn the language without the help of an interpreter. We must learn in the natural way, by observing the conduct and attending to the discourse of the citizens. For some simple words, colour words, for example, it will be fairly easy to make a dictionary. We can discover the word for 'blue' by noting what is said of the sky, forget-me-nots, bluebells, and the like. If all these things are called 'X', we can, with some confidence, write in our dictionary 'X=blue'; and our hypothesis may well be confirmed by later evidence of the same kind. There may, of course, be philosophical difficulties connected with this procedure, but in practice it, or something very much like it, will work well enough.

If we now proceed to more ambitious words, like 'rich', 'poor', 'employer', new difficulties may confront us. It may be impossible to get exact equivalents for such words in a foreign tongue, unless the alien society has a structure very like our own. But the general principle will hold good, for if there are equivalents, these can be obtained by noting the common characteristics of objects to which an unknown word applies. It is simply that, in these latter cases, what is common may be a matter of function, including social function. For example, if we want the word for 'king', we must first establish that the society is a monarchy, and then what a monarch is called. And there are likely to be difficulties, because the ruler of the country might exercise kingly powers, and yet the office might not be hereditary. Or there might be two persons, one of whom has the legal function of sovereignty, and the other the ceremonial function. In all such cases accurate translation is impossible, because the concepts, or word uses, in the two languages overlap. A substantial part of the philosophical vocabulary falls into this category. For example, the Attic Greek possesses at least half a dozen different words,[7] all of which are from time to time translated as 'know', and none of which means exactly what 'know' means in English. And this makes it very hard to convey, or even to understand, Greek theories of knowledge.

The other category of words, which is of interest here, consists of all such words as: good and bad (in the moral sense), tragic, comic, pleasant, repugnant, and the rest. It is useless to attempt applying the same methods to discovering equivalents for these words. For suppose we found that our foreigners applied the word 'X' to everything we found comical, and we wrote down 'comical=X'. We might very well be wrong, because they may have a different sense of humour. In order to find the word for 'comical', we have to see what they say about what makes them laugh, not what they say about what makes us laugh. Otherwise we may find ourselves committed to saying: These people know what is comic, and what is tragic, but they only laugh at tragic things. It would be as if they could see an event as really tragic, and yet be filled with amusement, with no hint of sorrow. And that seems quite absurd. Similar considerations apply to the identification of moral terms. If we want to know what words in the language express moral virtue, we must find out how people describe the actions and things that fill them with moral complacency; and if we want the expressions for moral evil, we must find out how they describe the actions and things that fill them with shame and remorse.

If this account is correct, it is easy to prove that words like 'virtuous', 'vicious', 'comical', and the like, cannot stand for any quality of actions or objects. This is true, even if there is some quality common to all virtuous things, or all comical things: even then, the words 'virtuous', 'comical' cannot stand for these qualities. For suppose we have two languages A and B. Making our dictionary for language A, we get 'X = red', 'Y=comical'. In language B we find 'Z=blue', 'T= comical'. As consequences of these findings, we then have X does not equal Z, and Y equals T. Now suppose the speakers of language A were accustomed to laugh at anything red, and only such things, so that anything described as X, they automatically describe as Y. The speakers of language B have a different (if equally curious) sense of humour: they laugh at blue things, and so everything described as Z is also described as T. If on these grounds we write X equals Y, and Z equals T, we shall have either X equals Z or Y does not equal T, contrary to our earlier findings. Hence, assuming those findings to be correct, we must conclude that either X does not equal Y or Z does not equal T. It is clear that identically similar considerations

apply to moral terms, and that the qualities X and Z may
be arbitrarily chosen. In particular, for any quality X we can
produce a hypothetical case where X equals not-Z, when it
follows both that X equals not-Y and Z equals not-T.

These arguments from hypothetical cases, no matter how
strange and unlikely such cases may be, do seem to constitute
a conclusive proof that moral virtue cannot be identified with
any quality of actions or things or persons. We can establish
in much the same way that the possession of moral virtue is
never entailed by the possession of any such quality, although
some further complications have to be allowed for here. But
we must remember that, although Hume held this position,
and although he was right (if what we have said is correct),
and although he may have had some such argument in mind,
the arguments he actually produces are persuasive, and not
conclusive. He brings people face to face with the problem
of deducing ought from is, or moral virtue from qualities, in
the hope that they will then feel it to be impossible, and so
become converted. He does not prove it is impossible.

The truth is that Hume had little interest in the ethical
problems which make people see virtue as an objective
quality, and moral goodness as something absolute and ultimate. The problems of moral improvement and of moral
decision, which for so many philosophers have been the
origin and motive forces of ethical speculation, were not felt
by him with the same overwhelming urgency.[8] Perhaps he
was content with his character, and had little difficulty in
making up his mind. He was not interested in moral questions as such, but rather in their natural history: not 'Is it
good?' but 'Why do people feel it to be good?'

II

Hume's position is that we have a sense of morals, just as we
have a sense of humour. The moral virtue of an action or
character lies wholly in the fact that it produces in spectators
a feeling of moral approval, just as the humour of an action
or situation lies wholly in the fact that it produces in spectators a feeling of merriment. And the feeling of moral approval

is immediately recognizable and incapable of further analysis, just as the feeling of merriment is immediately recognizable and incapable of further analysis. If this is accepted, the only remaining question seems to be: Is there any feature common to just those actions and characters which excite moral approval, and if so what is this feature? Hume discusses this question at considerable length, but with a regrettable lack of clarity. His conclusion appears to be that there is something common to all virtuous conduct, and this is the social utility of such conduct, and this in turn consists in the tendency of such conduct to maximize pleasure, in the general sense.[9] But this is not a matter of philosophy, and we may suspect that his conclusions are somewhat hastily drawn from an inadequate survey of the field of moral conduct.

There are, however, several other questions of much greater philosophical interest. One of these may be put in the following way. It may be admitted that there is some essential connexion, even an equivalence, between the moral virtue of an action and its capacity for producing moral approval in spectators. But, it may be asked, when we say 'This is morally good', do we mean (a) This produces moral approval in us, or (b) This would produce moral approval in anyone, or (c) This would produce moral approval in most people, or (d) This would produce moral approval in all persons of sound moral sentiment, or (e) This is approved by God, or (f) This merits our moral approval? We may suppose that Hume rejects the last three of these alternatives.[10] He often speaks as if he adopted the first alternative, that is the view that 'This is good' means 'I morally approve of this', but this is open to the obvious objection that if one person says a thing is good and another person says the same thing is not good, then they are not contradicting one another. For, on such a view, one person says he morally approves of the thing in question, and the other person says he does not. It is just as if one should say he likes oysters, and another that he does not. Of course, this is an objection only if we assume beforehand that, when people differ on moral questions, they really are contradicting one another. The second alternative, which Hume seems sometimes to have in mind, has the difficulty that there is scarcely anything which is approved by everyone without exception, and in fact we certainly do not demand this as a necessary condition of moral virtue. The third alternative seems the most plausible one, if we are thinking in Hume's terms. It is the democratic view of morals: what most people feel to be right *is* right. It is just possible that Hume sometimes inclines towards the fourth alternative, provided that 'sound moral sentiment' is not defined as 'capacity for accurate perception of what is good', for this would lead to circularity. What the theory amounts to, is that 'morally good' means 'approved by all members of a certain class', where membership of the class is determined by possession of certain previously specified *empirical* characteristics. Thus, the people qualified to pass moral judgements might be priests, rulers, all those of advanced age, all manual workers, or something of that kind. But if Hume adopts a theory of this sort, he does not attempt to specify the class of privileged persons.

That Hume does not define his position more precisely must not be taken as a fault or inadequacy in his theory of morals. All he wishes to say is that morals is a matter of taste, just as beauty is a matter of taste, humour is a matter of taste, and excellence in all the arts is a matter of taste. In all these cases we recognize that different people have different tastes, and that some people are more refined and judicious in their tastes than others. There is good taste and there is bad taste, and in all cases there are connoisseurs whose judgement we respect, even when it runs contrary to our own feelings. Hume does not, of course, mean that morals is a *mere* matter of taste, in the sense in which we often employ this phrase, meaning that it is a matter of no consequence, or that everyone is equally qualified to judge, and may follow his own feeling independently of the feelings of others. There may be a philosophical problem about the objectivity of judgements of taste, but if Hume is right this problem is not peculiar to moral judgements. Many philosophers have held the view that there is something peculiar to moral judgements, which

sets them apart from other matters of taste, and which leads
to a special kind of philosophical problem. Hume tries to
show that this view is wrong, and that in this connexion at
least, there is no special problem of moral philosophy.

There are two other matters which many people hold to be
especially important in moral philosophy. These are the
problems of the existence and nature of God, and the problem of free-will. The existence and nature of God is felt to be
important for morals, because moral virtue is sometimes defined as what is pleasing to God, and because he is often invoked to rectify the imperfections of earthly justice. The concept of free-will is felt to be important, because it seems that
we only praise or blame a person for his conduct when we
believe him to be acting in some sense as a free agent. Hume's
position is that both the existence and nature of God, and the
concept of free-will are irrelevant to morals. We now take
this opportunity to give some account of Hume's attitude to
religion in general, and to the relation between religion and
morals.

Hume's reflections on religion take the form of a dialogue
between three characters, Demea, Cleanthes, and Philo.[11]
Demea maintains that the existence of God is certain and
self-evident, and also that it is the object of *a priori* proof. But
he says that God's nature and attributes are both unknowable and inconceivable by human beings. Cleanthes bases
himself on what is called 'the argument from design', that is
to say, he points out that the natural world exhibits notable
evidence of order and design, and so there must be a designer.
Philo has no positive views: his function is to clarify and
criticize the suggestions made by the others. The object of his
criticism is not simply refutation: he also facilitates modifica-
tion and further elaboration of the views proposed.

Although the disputants formally state that the existence
of God is not in question, this must not be taken seriously. A
substantial part of the dialogue is in fact concerned with the
question of existence, and, indeed, it is hard to see how the
question of God's nature and attributes could be discussed
independently. For it seems that the question of the existence

of God cannot be other than a question of the existence of something having certain antecedently specified characteristics, and our analysis will be simplified if we first state what these are. We may take it for granted that Hume's discussion is carried on in the context of Christianity, or some similar religion. In such religions God is associated with the following functions: (1) Creation of the natural world, (2) Moral government of human beings, (3) Concern for the happiness and well-being of humanity, (4) The object of human adoration and worship. By moral government we mean that one of God's functions is to watch over the conduct of human beings, rewarding the virtuous and punishing evildoers, according to their deserts, possibly in an after-life. He is regarded as the final court of appeal in moral matters, and his judgement is absolutely binding. In addition to the four functions set out above, God is supposed to have a further characteristic, namely that of absolute perfection. Possession of this characteristic is the starting point for the so-called ontological proof of the existence of God.

It is not obvious that possession of any one or more of these functions and qualities entails possession of any of the others. There is nothing to suggest, for example, that the creator of the world must necessarily be its moral governor, or that he must be absolutely perfect. It seems that the various functions might well be performed by distinct beings, and this is in fact the view held in some non-Christian religions. In primitive religions, especially, the creator god is not an object of worship, and those gods who are objects of worship often take little account of the morality of their worshippers.[12] Consequently, if we define God as a being having all five of these characteristics, then a proof of his existence must either be a proof that some being has all five characteristics, or a proof that some being has one or more of them, and that possession of the others is consequent on this. We can now see some possible confusions and difficulties in religious discussion. For example, we might accept some proof that there is a creator of the natural world, and we might even agree that this creator is concerned for the happiness and well-being of mankind. But since the happiness of mankind is far from perfect, it seems that the creator cannot be absolutely perfect. If he is willing to make us all happy, he is incapable of doing so; and if he is capable of doing so, he is unwilling. This conclusion may be avoided, either by saying, in the teeth of the evidence, that the world is perfect, or by saying that here is a mystery too deep for human understanding. And whatever we may think of the first of these suggestions, the second certainly cannot be rejected out of hand by any reasonable person. In the same way, an absolutely perfect being is hard to reconcile with the moral governor of mankind, for the virtuous are not invariably rewarded nor the wicked punished. It thus seems that either God's judgement is sometimes at fault, or else he is sometimes unwilling or unable to execute that judgement. This conclusion is, of course, often avoided by saying that the obvious injustices of this life are rectified in an after-life, or by claiming that virtue is its own reward and wickedness its own punishment. One of these alternatives is hard to assess, the other is hard to understand.

As might be expected, Hume's conclusions in these matters are entirely sceptical. He thinks that the ontological argument is certainly fallacious because existence is not a predicate.[13] Of the argument from design, he says that the most that can be gleaned from it is 'that the cause or causes of order in the universe probably bear some remote analogy to human intelligence'. There is nothing to suggest that God is benevolently disposed towards mankind, or that he is interested in the morality of our conduct. But the most interesting feature of Hume's treatment of religion is his abandonment of his usual analytical method. Judging by the methods employed in the *Treatise*, we should have expected him first to have considered the meaning of the word 'God'.[14] If this word has meaning, it must, according to Hume, stand for some idea, and there must be some possible impression corresponding to this idea. Furthermore, if the idea of God is a simple idea, we must already have had the simple impression corresponding to it. That is to say we must have seen God. If the idea of God is a complex idea, then we have to account for how people come to believe in the existence of the impression corresponding to this complex idea. Then we should have expected Hume to give some account of the origin of our belief in the existence of God, independently of the truth of that belief. In short, we should have expected his treatment of God to follow the lines laid down in his treatment of causation, the material world, and the self. But he does not attempt this. All he does is to consider some ancient arguments for the existence of God, and expose their weaknesses, and conclude that belief in God is not rationally founded. He does this in the other cases too, but there he goes on to explain how people acquire a belief which is not rationally founded, and this is the most interesting and original part of his work. Thus Hume's treatment of religion is disappointing, since it is only a prolegomena to a full treatment on Humean lines. It is hard to see what caused him to miss this opportunity for contributing something really original to natural religion.

The concept of God is related to moral philosophy in two ways. First, it may be said that 'good' means 'pleasing to God', or something of that kind. Second, it may be said that belief in the existence of God is a necessary support of human morality. We have seen that Hume denies the first of these propositions. He also denies the second, on the empirical ground that many virtuous people have rejected either the existence of God or his interest in the morality of our conduct. Some further analysis of these points will be of interest.

At first sight, the question whether 'good' means 'pleasing to God' is a question, not of philosophy, but of philology. When English people use the word 'good' do they mean the same as when they use the phrase 'pleasing to God'? Now we can easily establish that when *some* English people use 'good' they do *not* mean 'pleasing to God'. Atheists, for example, often assert that a thing is good, and at the same time deny that it is pleasing to God, because, they say, there is no God. On the other hand, there is nothing to prevent some other people, Christians, for example, from using 'good' to mean 'pleasing to God'. And, of course, there is nothing to prevent some other people from using 'good' to mean 'displeasing to God', or 'pleasing to pigs', or anything else you care to think of. The question then is, do all these people mean the same thing by 'good'? If they do, we can say they have different metaphysical theories about the nature of good. If they do not, there is obviously no quarrel.

Now it might seem that these people could not possibly all mean the same thing by 'good', but it is just at this point that we have to be exceptionally clear-headed. For it could be the case that all these people applied the word 'good' to exactly the same things, and even that they all had the same attitude to the things they described as good. They might all agree, not only about what things are good, but also that good things merit praise and reward. If this were the case, it does seem that they would all mean the same by 'good', but would differ in their opinions as to the metaphysical nature of goodness. Such a conclusion is supported by the fact that, if we wish to ascertain the synonym for 'good' in an unknown language, we try to find out how the users of that language describe those things which they praise and reward.

Now, if this is so, we are bound to ask how people differ when they differ about the nature of good. They all agree about what things are good, and that good things merit praise and reward, and yet one says what is good is what is pleasing to God, another that what is good is what is pleasing to most human beings, another that what is good is what is pleasing to pigs, another that what is good is what maximizes human happiness, and so on. The content of their disagreement is obvious enough: they agree about what is meant by 'good', but they have *different methods* for finding out what is good. One tells us to praise, practise, and encourage what is pleasing to God, another to praise, practise, and encourage what pleases most human beings, and so on. If these different methods all give the same results, there need be no difficulty. But it is plain that, although these methods may all give the same results, they need not do so. If they do not, it seems that we should have to ask ourselves which method is the right one. This may very well be the central question of moral philosophy.

The question which moral decision method is the right one is a question of which method gives correct results. And this is a question of the function of moral conduct, the purpose it serves. This is where morality differs from humour. The function of humour is to excite feelings of merriment, but it is not the *function* of moral conduct to excite feelings of moral approval. Hume recognizes this, for he examines at some length the kinds of conduct which excite moral approval, and concludes that generally speaking they are the kinds of conduct which tend to increase human happiness. But by moral conduct he means conduct which excites moral approval, and so for him it is only an accident that moral conduct has this function of increasing human happiness. It might have been the case that moral conduct increased human misery, or even tended to extinguish the human race altogether. All this is part of Hume's general policy for expelling necessary but unintelligible connexions in favour of the accidental yet ineluctable sequences of the natural world. Evidently, if the function of moral conduct is accidental, it may well be part of its function to please God. There is nothing in Hume's theory against the hypothesis.[15] He would only say there is no evidence for it, and it is not demonstrable.

There are other difficulties in Hume's theory, much more difficult to state, and involving the question of free-will. A little preliminary discussion of this concept will be helpful. The problem of free-will is a comparatively late development in philosophy, it is not one of the primary questions which have puzzled all contemplative men at all times. It becomes apparent only in the context of a well-developed ethical religion, or of a well-developed science of nature. If God is not thought of as a moral governor, the question of his moral standing in relation to his puppets is not an urgent one. If natural events are viewed as the work of anthropomorphic powers, there is nothing disturbing in the analogy between the works of nature and the deeds of men. But if God is omnipotent, it seems odd, to say the least, that he should punish his creatures for their misdeeds. It is as if someone should rebuke a servant who carried out his commands. And if we no longer pass moral judgement on trees and stones, why should we do so on our fellow men, who are equally bound by natural laws?

The theological problem is put by Hume in a slightly different form: If God is omnipotent he is responsible for all the evil in the world, and if God is responsible for evil he is not morally perfect.[16] Therefore, either there is no evil in the world, or God is not omnipotent, or he is not morally perfect. Evidently there is a problem, only if you feel bound to maintain that there is evil in the world, that God is omnipotent, and that he is morally perfect. Hume seems to admit there is a problem, but he declines to deal with it on the ground that its solution is outside the power of the human intellect. But his attitude to questions of this sort is a little ambiguous, and it may well be that he would reject one or more of the three propositions involved.

The scientific problem finds him much more sure of himself. He maintains that the actions and thoughts of men are entirely subject to natural laws, and in this respect there is no essential difference between men and animals, or between animals and inanimate objects. He supports his position with numerous persuasive examples of the uniformity and predictability of human actions.[17] But he reminds us that, when we say A necessitates B, or that if A happens B is bound to happen, all we can mean is that B always follows A, or that having seen A we feel inclined to expect B. We have no idea of a necessary connexion between objects. Consequently, when we say men are bound by natural laws, we simply mean their behaviour follows a pattern, and that we can and do sometimes correctly forecast such behaviour. Even when a man acts, as it seems to him, according to the free and unconstrained dictates of his will, it is true that an acute and experienced observer can forecast what he does. And the fact that a man always behaves badly, so that we come to expect him to behave badly, does not by itself prevent us from condemning him. The incorrigible rogue is still a rogue. The fact that a man always and infallibly behaves well increases rather than diminishes our respect for him. It thus seems that the predictability of conduct does not affect our moral judgement of it.

There is one other possible connexion between religion and morals. It has been suggested that religious belief is an indispensable support of morality; that is to say, people would not behave well unless they were influenced by fears of the wrath of God, vengeance in a life after death, or something of that sort. This has nothing to do with the truth of such beliefs. Since Hume's position is that the moral sentiment exists in human nature independently of religion, he naturally denies that religious belief is essential for morality. He cites in his support various famous infidels who have been notably moral men. But the question is really much more complicated and difficult than he seems to think. It is, however, a factual, not a philosophical question.

CHAPTER 6

THE NATURE OF THINGS

I

THE basic entities in Hume's philosophy are what he calls 'perceptions of the mind'. We have considered some of the features attributed to these objects, but two outstanding questions remain to be determined. These are: How are perceptions related to material objects, such as apples and elephants? and: How are perceptions related to the mind or soul which perceives them? Hume gives his answers in the fourth book of the *Treatise of Human Nature*, and our present object is to examine what he has to say in this connexion. But before we try to do this, it will be convenient to review the part played by perceptions in his general theory.

The first thing to grasp is Hume's account of the meaning of a word. He says the meaning of a word is the idea which it expresses, or for which it stands; and a word has meaning only if it expresses an idea. General terms, like 'apple' or 'triangle', do not of course stand for particular ideas,[1] that is to say, they do not always stand for the same idea on every occasion of their use. Rather, they express, as it were ambiguously, any one of a number of different ideas. But we may speak without confusion of the idea of a triangle, so long as we remember that we mean by this some arbitrary representative of the numerous different ideas of triangles – isosceles triangles, equilateral triangles, and the rest. Furthermore, in order to use the word 'triangle' meaningfully, it is not necessary that we should have in mind at the time of speaking any particular idea of any particular triangle, but it *is* necessary that we could have such an idea if we chose to. Thus, in any case, a word cannot have meaning unless there is, or could be, at least one idea for which it stands. Moreover, every idea is a copy of some possible impression. It follows that a word can have meaning only if it stands for an idea, which is in turn a copy of some possible impression. In view of the intimate relation between ideas and impressions we can say in short that a word has meaning only if it stands for some possible impression. The final point is that simple ideas must always be preceded by the corresponding simple impression. Consequently, if a word stands for a simple impression, we must have had that simple impression. There is no doubt that, in giving this account of meaning, Hume was thinking principally of nouns and adjectives. The theory is very difficult to apply to other words, even adverbs.

If this theory is correct, it follows that words like 'apple', 'elephant', 'mind' are either meaningless, or they stand for impressions. Hume takes it for granted that the first two of these words do mean something; his attitude to the third is hard to determine. But if 'apple' and 'elephant' stand for impressions, then apples and elephants must *be* impressions. In general, material objects and real events are impressions, and so they are a kind of perceptions. This is in fact the view tacitly adopted by Hume in his treatment of causation. The apparently contradictory nature of this identification is at once revealed if we compare the features attributed by Hume to perceptions with the features commonly attributed to material objects. Concerning perceptions, we have: (1) perceptions exist only when they appear to the mind, (2) they are always just as they seem, (3) they cannot change, (4) they are private. The corresponding features commonly attributed to material objects are: (1) they exist even when not perceived, (2) they are not always as they seem, (3) they can change, (4) they are not private. If we assume that both these ascriptions are correct, it follows that material objects are not perceptions. Furthermore, if the word 'apple' is meaningful, apples must be perceptions; and so apples cannot be material objects, and they cannot possess the characteristic features of material objects.

This argument does not, of course, prove that apples are not material objects, since one of the premisses may be false. What is established beyond doubt is that *at most four* of the following five statements can be true:

(1) Perceptions exist only when perceived, etc.
(2) Material objects exist when not perceived, etc.
(3) The word 'apple' is meaningful.
(4) If 'apple' is meaningful, then apples are perceptions.
(5) Apples are material objects.

In order to preserve logical consistency, Hume must reject one of these statements, and he need not reject more than one. On the other hand, it does seem that if he rejects any one, he must either abandon his own principles [expressed in (1) and (4)], or abandon the opinions of common sense [expressed in (2), (3), and (5)]. In fact he rejects (2), and concludes that material objects do not continue to exist when unperceived. The belief that they do, is a kind of illusion.

It is important to understand that Hume could have avoided his difficulty in another way. He could have rejected the first statement in the list. He could have said that perceptions, or some of them, do continue to exist when unperceived, do sometimes appear other than they really are, and in short have all the characteristics commonly attributed to material objects. Although I have suggested that this would be contrary to his principles, it is so only in a relative sense. It does not transgress, as it were, his ultimate terms of reference. It is not part of Hume's definition of perceptions, that they should be 'internal and perishing existences', and that they should 'appear in every particular what they are, and be what they appear'. These may be definitive of the modern concept of sense-datum, but they are not definitive of Hume's perceptions. For him, a perception is anything which 'appears to the mind', and nothing whatever follows from this about the other features of such entities. Confusion arises because Hume does speak as if the fact that they 'appear in every particular' were partly definitive of perceptions. But this is a piece of carelessness, and it is not an essential feature of his theory. The fact that perceptions are 'internal and perishing existences' is explicitly treated by him as a matter of fact, and not as a matter of definition. Consequently, he could have rejected the first statement listed in the previous paragraph without damaging his basic principles. And if he had rejected that statement, he could have preserved the truth of common-sense beliefs about material objects.

We may very well ask why Hume did not take this course. The answer to this question is both complicated and obscure: it is part of a more general question about the historical origins of philosophical empiricism. We cannot answer it here, but we may make one negative observation. It was not that Hume was prejudiced against common sense. On the contrary, he was all in favour of common sense, and took the greatest trouble to come to terms with it, in his own peculiar way. By this I mean that although Hume thought that some common-sense beliefs are false, he did not make the mistake of supposing that they should, or could, be abandoned. Hume's attitude to common sense was, I think, unique in the history of philosophy.[3] He was utterly opposed to the ancient tradition of high philosophy, which regarded common-sense beliefs as a kind of popular fallacies, it being the business of philosophers to expose and correct these fallacies, and ultimately to transcend them. On the other hand, he would have been equally opposed to the modern view, which seems to have first been suggested by Thomas Reid.[4] In this view the beliefs of common sense are regarded as the very measure of truth, so that any philosophical statement which conflicts with common sense is for that reason rejected as false. An unjustifiable contempt for common sense has been replaced by an equally unjustifiable veneration.

Hume's position in this matter is still not entirely clear to us. We must first try to see why he concludes that our belief in the continued existence of material objects is a false belief. Then we must follow his explanation of how we come to acquire this false belief. Lastly, we must ask why we cannot abandon this belief, even when we have been convinced by philosophical argument of its falsity. This last question is very important, for it would seem on the face of it that any answer must make a sharp distinction between natural belief and philosophical conviction, a distinction which will lead

Hume back to the old rationalist distinction between the two sorts of knowledge.

Hume starts by observing that common sense makes no distinction between a perception and the material object we are ordinarily said to perceive. He says:[5]

'Tis certain that almost all mankind, and even philosophers themselves, for the greatest part of their lives, take their perceptions to be their only objects, and suppose, that the very being, which is intimately present to the mind, is the real body or material existence. 'Tis also certain, that this very perception or object is supposed to have a continued uninterrupted being, and neither to be annihilated by our absence, nor to be brought into existence by our presence. When we are absent from it, we say it still exists, but that we do not feel, we do not see it. When we are present, we say we feel, or see it.

This, then, is the common-sense belief: not merely that material objects continue to exist unperceived, but also that some perceptions, at least, are material objects. Hume places great stress on this latter point:[6]

The very image, which is present to the senses, is with us the real body; and 'tis to these interrupted images we ascribe a perfect identity.

The vulgar confound perceptions and objects, and attribute a distinct continued existence to the very things they feel or see.

'Tis indeed evident, that as the vulgar suppose their perceptions to be their only objects, and at the same time believe the continued existence of matter, we must account for the origin of the belief upon that assumption.

There are many other passages to the same effect. Hume is anxious to get this clear, because he is aware that many people hold a causal theory of perception. That is to say, they believe that material objects are not themselves perceptions, but that they are capable of causing perceptions under suitable conditions. This is not the common-sense view; it is a metaphysical, or at best a quasi-scientific theory, and a false theory according to Hume. Its truth would entail the falsity of one of his basic principles, namely his principle of meaning.

The next point is that perceptions do not have a continued and independent existence. That is to say, they do not exist when they are not perceived. I have already pointed out that this is not a matter of logical necessity for Hume; indeed, it cannot be so, if his account of the origin of common-sense beliefs is to be workable. His arguments may be summed up as follows. First, perceptions may change, although the material object which they are perceptions of does not change.[7] Or, more accurately, two quite different perceptions may be perceptions of the same material object, even when that object has not changed at all. For example, we see a tower, first at a distance, and then close up. The tower has not changed at all, although the two perceptions are widely different. Second, we do not ascribe continued existence to all our perceptions, but only to those which we identify with material objects. We say apples continue to exist when not perceived, but we say that headaches, or feelings of anger, do not continue to exist when not perceived. We must analyse these arguments as carefully as we can, for their importance is by no means restricted to the use Hume makes of them.

What the first argument proves is that if the tower did not change, then at least one of the perceptions cannot be identical with the tower. It does *not* prove that neither of the perceptions is identical with the tower. Indeed, the ancient solution of this problem (it is an ancient problem) consisted in saying that the close-up view was when you really saw the tower.[8] In order to get the stronger conclusion, one must establish the additional premiss: that if either one of the perceptions is not identical with the tower, then neither perception is identical with the tower. So far as I know, no valid proof of this premiss has ever been given. What has been said is that, since there is no method for deciding which perception is identical with the tower, and one is not, neither can be. The reader will see that this is not a valid argument in the ordinary acceptance of the term. It is, perhaps, an attempt to persuade. But even if we are persuaded, what is proved is not that the tower is distinct from both perceptions, but only that if the tower has not changed it must be distinct from both perceptions. It may be common sense to say the tower has not changed. But then it is also common sense to say that what we perceive is the tower. What the argument appears to prove is that at least one of these common-sense beliefs must be false, and should be abandoned. It does not enable us to decide which of the beliefs is false. And no conclusion follows as to the continued existence or otherwise of perceptions.

The other point made by Hume is that we do not ascribe continued existence to all our perceptions, but only to those which we identify with material objects.[9] Headaches, feelings of anger, and ideas of every kind exist, according to common sense, only when perceived. We must again observe that it does not immediately follow that no perceptions have a continued existence. The only conclusion we are entitled to draw is that, if common sense is wrong on this point, then either no perceptions have a continued existence, or they all do. Now Hume gives no argument or persuasive indication that common sense is wrong on this point. But he certainly believes that it is wrong, and we must try to conjecture what may have led him to this position.

Berkeley, and many others, have held that common sense must be wrong, because it is logically impossible for perceptions to exist when unperceived.[10] We have been over this before, and all we need notice here is that Hume does not, and cannot consistently, hold this view. For he says we do believe that perceptions have continued existences, or that some of them do, that we can believe only what we can imagine, and that we can imagine only what is possible. Such is his position: its difficulties in other connexions need not concern us here. It is not logically impossible for perceptions to continue to exist unperceived. Thus, he says:[11]

An interrupted appearance to the senses implies not necessarily an interruption in the existence. The supposition of the continued existence of sensible objects or perceptions involves no contradiction. We may easily indulge our inclination to that supposition.

Evidently, his reasons for saying no perceptions do in fact have such continued existence must be sought along other lines.

It will be remembered that Hume's principal object here is to explain how we come to believe in the continued existence of some perceptions, and not of others. We must now consider this explanation. Hume says that perceptions to which we ascribe continued existence, that is to say, perceptions of material objects, are characterized by their *constancy* and their *coherence*. We cannot improve upon his own descriptions of these features:[12]

All those objects to which we attribute a continued existence, have a peculiar *constancy*, which distinguishes them from the impressions, whose existence depends upon our perception. Those mountains, and houses, and trees, which lie at present under my eye, have always appeared to me in the same order; and when I lose sight of them by shutting my eyes or turning my head, I soon after find them return upon me without the least alteration. My bed and table, my books and papers, present themselves in the same uniform manner, and change not upon account of any interruption in my seeing or perceiving them. This is the case with all the impressions, whose objects are supposed to have an external existence; and is the case with no other impressions, whether gentle or violent, voluntary or involuntary.

The constancy is not invariable, and so coherence is also required:

Bodies often change their position and qualities, and after a little absence or interruption may become hardly knowable. But here 'tis observable, that even in these changes they preserve a *coherence*, and have a regular dependence on each other; which is the foundation of a kind of reasoning from causation, and produces the opinion of their continued existence. When I return to my chamber after an hour's absence, I find not my fire in the same situation, in which I left it: But then I am accustomed in other instances to see a like alteration produced in a like time, whether I am present or absent, near or remote. This coherence, therefore, in their changes is one of the characteristics of external objects, as well as their constancy.

Hume thinks that these are the only characteristics peculiar to our perceptions of material objects. It is natural to suppose that they must somehow cause our belief in the continued existence of such objects when unperceived. His next task is to give a plausible account of how this occurs.

It is important for Hume that he should be able to give some sort of account of how the constancy and coherence of perceptions gives rise to our belief in their continued existence. The exact nature of his story is not so important, although of course it must not transgress his basic principles, and it must possess a certain kind of plausibility. We summarize what he has to say.[13] To begin with coherence, it will be remembered that, after we have perceived A followed by B on several occasions, we come to expect B on perceiving A. But if, when we perceive A, we instantly shut our eyes, or turn our heads away, or something of the sort, we shall not perceive B. The natural consequence of previous observations, however, will lead us to believe that B must have occurred, but unperceived. The explanation for this phenomenon is that, once having observed a regularity of sequence between A and B, we naturally tend to preserve this regularity in the face of seemingly contrary instances. We do this by saying that the seemingly contrary instance was not really contrary, because B really did occur in this case, although it was not observed to occur. The matter is really much more complicated than it appears by this account, but there is no reason to suppose that Hume could not have dealt with the additional complexities, had he undertaken to do so.

The part played by constancy of perceptions is as follows. If we have a perception, and then later have the same perception again, it seems natural to conclude that it must have existed between whiles. For how else could it be the same? It follows that such a perception must continue to exist when unperceived. Hume's position is that this is indeed what makes us believe that the perception continues to exist when unperceived, but it does not constitute a proof that such is the case. It is not a proof, because our reasoning depends upon a confusion of two different meanings of the phrase 'the same'.[14] In general, we may say, for example, that we are in the same house today as we were yesterday. By this, we mean the same identical house, Number 12 Acacia Gardens, or whatever it might be. This kind of sameness is often called *numerical identity*. On the other hand, we may say the doctor gave A and B the same treatment, meaning only that the treatment he gave A is exactly like the treatment he gave B. This kind of sameness is sometimes called *qualitative identity*, in order to distinguish it from numerical identity. Evidently John Jones can be numerically identical only with John Jones, but John Jones may be qualitatively identical with Peter Jones, if they happen for example to be identical twins. Now it is obvious that the conclusion that a perception exists when unperceived holds only if what is later perceived is numerically identical with what is earlier perceived. But all we are really entitled to say, is that what is later perceived is qualitatively identical with what is earlier perceived. Consequently our instinctive argument is unwarranted, and depends for its apparent force on confusing qualitative identity with numerical identity. It is because of this confusion that the constancy of certain perceptions leads to a belief in their continued existence.

The important fact to grasp is that Hume's account of how we come to believe in the continued existence of some perceptions is perfectly compatible with the fact, if it is a fact, that they do not have such existence. His story of the origin of such beliefs by no means entails their truth. We must now return to our earlier question, and ask how Hume comes by the opinion that perceptions are 'interrupted and perishing existences'. He makes first a distinction between the continued existence of perceptions and their independent existence. The precise nature of this distinction need not concern us at present. All we need to know is that continued existence entails independent existence, and that therefore lack of independent existence entails lack of continued existence. He then proceeds:[15]

'Twill first be proper to observe a few of those experiments which convince us, that our perceptions are not possesst of any independent existence. When we press one eye with a finger, we immediately perceive all the objects to become double, and one half of them to be removed from their common and natural position. But as we do not attribute a continued existence to both these perceptions, and as they are both of the same nature, we clearly perceive, that all our perceptions are dependent on our organs, and the disposition of our nerves and animal spirits. This opinion is confirmed by the seeming increase and diminution of objects, according to their distance; by the apparent alterations in their figure; by the changes in their colour and other qualities from our sickness and distempers; and by an infinite number of other experiments of the same kind; from all of which we learn, that our sensible perceptions are not possest of any distinct or independent existence.

There is no doubt that some such observations serve to convince us of the interrupted and perishing nature of perceptions, even our perceptions of material objects. And judging by his use of the phrase 'we clearly perceive' for the inference here, he is ready to view it as a straightforward piece of deductive reasoning. But a careful reading of the passage will soon convince the reader that the reasoning involved cannot be deductive. The observations specified no more entail the perishing nature of perceptions, than coherence and constancy entail the opposite. The two cases are really exactly on a level: the coherence and constancy of perceptions leads us to believe that they do continue to exist unperceived, double images and the rest lead us to believe that perceptions do not continue to exist when unperceived. In neither case is the conclusion a logical consequence of the observations. The truth is that every possible perceptual phenomenon is compatible with both of these contradictory assertions.

Hume's true position must therefore be somewhat as follows. First, human nature is such that certain features of perceptual experience, which do in fact occur, cause human beings to believe that some perceptions continue to exist when unperceived. Second, human nature is such that certain other features of perceptual experience, which also occur in fact, cause human beings to believe that these same perceptions do not continue to exist when unperceived. Third, because our nature is what it is, we cannot abandon either of these beliefs, although they are plainly contradictory. Fourth, as to whether perceptions do or do not continue to exist when unperceived, we can have no direct information.[16]

The question which immediately raises itself is: how, and in what sense, can we hold two contradictory beliefs? There are some obvious senses in which this is possible. First, if two beliefs are not known to be contradictory, or if they are believed to be compatible, we can, of course, entertain them both. We sometimes make mistakes in logic. This can hardly be so in the present case, however, for our two beliefs about perceptions are plainly contradictory. Second, we can hold one belief at one time, and another contradictory belief at some later time. Thus we may at one time believe that all swans are white, and later experience teaches us that this is not so. The analogy here is a little stronger, but it will not bear examination. For when we are convinced that perceptions do not have continued existence, we do not, according to Hume, abandon our former belief that they do have continued existence. We cannot abandon it. Perhaps a better analogy is one with which we have become familiar through recent developments in psychology. We know now that people may be driven by sentiments of desire or aversion into embracing both of two conflicting beliefs. In such cases only one such belief occupies the attention of the subject at any one time, but a different one according to circumstances. Questions of love, money, and politics supply us with innumerable examples of this sort of thing. We are often lured into believing that we can have our cake, and eat it too.

This last analogy is the strongest, but we must not press it too far. There are two points where it seems to fail. First, we must remember that, although it is our desire to have our cake and eat it which leads us to believe that we can have it and eat it, it is not our desire that perceptions should both continue to exist and not continue to exist when unperceived. Second, and more important, Hume does seem to think there is a sort of difference in status between our belief in the continued existence of perceptions, and our belief that they do not continue to exist. He thinks the former is in some sense stronger than the latter, although in what sense it is hard to say. Apart from these differences the analogy with wishful thinking is fair enough.

We now summarize what Hume has said so far. First, we cannot imagine, or believe in the existence of, anything except perceptions. Second, perceptions may or may not continue to exist when unperceived, and we have no direct means of deciding whether they do or no. Third, certain perceptions are identified with material objects, we believe that there are material objects, and that they continue to exist unperceived. Consequently we believe that some perceptions have such continued existence. This belief is engendered by the coherence and constancy of such perceptions. Certain other phenomena engender the belief that these same perceptions do not have continued existence. We are constrained to both these conflicting beliefs, but more strongly to the first. Every perceptual phenomenon is logically compatible with both beliefs, and the truth of the matter is not accessible to us. That is to say, everyone is bound to believe in a physical world, which exists independently of his awareness of it, but the truth of this belief can be neither proved nor disproved. Perceptions are the only things whose existence is accessible to the human understanding, and we cannot even imagine the existence of anything else.[17]

II

We now proceed to consider Hume's theory concerning the mind, or perceiving entity. It is important to understand that throughout this discussion he is interested in the mind as that which perceives, and not as that which supposedly governs the movements of the body. For this reason, he gives little attention to what many philosophers have regarded as the most important philosophical problem about the mind, namely the problem of how that which perceives can also govern the movements of the physical body. Instead, he considers first the problem of how perceptions are related to the mind which perceives them, and second, a rather curious and elusive problem, which he calls the problem of *personal identity*.

There are three theories about the relation of the mind to its perceptions, all based on physical analogies. In the first theory the mind is like a house, and the perceptions like inhabitants. Thus the house remains the same, even if its inhabitants change, and it remains in existence, even if it becomes uninhabited. Moreover, the inhabitants of the house may continue to exist, even if they leave the house, and they may take up residence elsewhere, or they may not live in a house at all. In the second theory the mind is like the sea, and perceptions are like waves in the sea. Here again the sea remains the same, even if the waves change, and the sea may continue to exist when there are no waves in it. On the other hand, the waves cannot leave the sea and exist by themselves, or in some other sea. Waves in different seas are different waves. In the third theory the mind is like a cloud, and perceptions are like the water-particles in a cloud. A cloud is nothing but a collection of water-particles, and so it cannot exist in the absence of the water-particles. The latter can, however, leave the cloud and exist apart from it. Furthermore, water-particles are always leaving the cloud, and new ones entering it, so that in a little time the whole constitution of the cloud is changed. Nevertheless, it remains, in a certain sense, the same cloud.

Hume uses the three words 'soul', 'mind', 'self' interchangeably, and it is clear that he thinks these words are meaningful. In accordance with his general principles, therefore, we should expect him to maintain that, since 'mind' is meaningful, the mind is a perception. That is to say, the mind perceives itself, amongst other things. There is nothing obviously illogical about this, it would be a theory of the first kind listed in the previous paragraph. Nonetheless, we find Hume taking special pains to say that the mind is *not* one perception amongst others. We must consider the arguments he produces in favour of this unexpected conclusion, a conclusion which on the face of it refutes one of the basic principles of his philosophy.[18] His first argument is that the mind or self 'is not any one impression, but that to which our several impressions and ideas are suppos'd to have a reference'. The suppressed premiss is, of course, that that to which impressions have a reference cannot be an impression. Or, in more familiar terms, that that which perceives cannot be perceived. This amounts to saying the perceptual relation is asymmetrical, a statement which itself demands proof. No proof is given, and the argument is therefore inconclusive. Hume's second argument is that, if we did perceive the self, this perception would remain the same throughout our lives, and no perception we have remains the same throughout our lives. Therefore we do not perceive the self or mind. It must be noted that this argument requires the purely empirical, factual premisses that no perception remains the same throughout our lives. It thus establishes at best that we do not in fact perceive the mind, and not that this is logically impossible. The other premiss of this argument also demands attention, namely the statement that if the self or mind is a perception, it must be a perception which remains the same throughout our lives. This is really the assumption that the self is an unchanging entity, and we shall comment upon it at a later stage. Hume's third argument consists simply in the statement that he has never succeeded in perceiving himself (that is, his mind), together with an explicit refusal to admit the claims of those who do claim to perceive themselves. This is, of course, an argument only in a very elastic sense of the term.

Hume concludes from these arguments that the mind cannot be identified with any one of its perceptions. On the other hand, the mind cannot be an unperceivable entity, different from any kind of perception, for on Hume's principles to say the mind is an unperceivable entity is to say the word 'mind' is meaningless. And the word 'mind' is not meaningless. His way out of this apparent contradiction is to say that the mind consists of the sum of its perceptions. In other words, he follows the third of the physical analogies set out above. For him, the mind is like a cloud, and its perceptions are like the water-particles that constitute a cloud. We are, he says, 'nothing but a bundle or collection of different perceptions', and we cease to exist when we cease to perceive.[19]

Now it is clear that two water-particles may be in the same cloud, or in different clouds. Likewise, two distinct perceptions may be in the same mind, or in different minds. Furthermore, what make two water-particles in the same cloud is a certain spatial proximity, or in other words, two particles are in the same cloud if either the distance between them does not exceed a certain maximum or there is a third particle in the same cloud as both.[20] But it is not in the least clear what is the corresponding relation between perceptions, which makes them constituents of the same mind. It cannot be a spatial relation because, as Hume himself points out, perceptions are not generally speaking spatially related. A feeling of anger is neither to the right nor to the left of the taste of an apple. Now it must be stressed that the problem of what it is that makes two perceptions members of the same mind is an extremely difficult one for Hume, and in the end he confesses himself baffled. I shall first try to summarize what he has to say. The reader must not be alarmed if he finds it unintelligible.

The first thing that Hume says is that we have to decide whether the relation is 'something that really binds our several perceptions together, or only associates their ideas in the imagination'. He concludes that, since 'the understanding never observes any real connexion among objects (sc. perceptions)',[21] it follows that 'identity is nothing really belonging to these different perceptions, and uniting them together; but is merely a quality, which we attribute to them, because of the union of their ideas in the imagination, when we reflect upon them.' Then he observes that the only qualities which associate ideas in the imagination are resemblance, contiguity, and causation, and it is in fact the function of these relations to produce an association of ideas, so that we proceed easily from one idea to another associated with it. Then he concludes 'it follows, that our notions of personal identity, proceed entirely from the smooth and uninterrupted progress of the thought along a train of connected ideas, according to the principles above explained.' The relation of resemblance operates to produce the notion of the self, through the medium of *memory*, 'For', Hume says, 'what is the memory but a faculty, by which we raise up the images of past perceptions? And as an image necessarily resembles its object, must not the frequent placing of these resembling perceptions in the chain of thought, convey the imagination more easily from one link to another, and make the whole seem like the continuance of one object?' As to the relation of causation, he says 'we may observe, that the true idea of the human mind, is to consider it as a system of different perceptions or different existences, which are linked together by the relation of cause and effect, and mutually produce, destroy, influence, and modify each other.'

In order to understand what is happening here, we must reconsider the questions Hume supposes himself to be answering. The first question arises out of a notion we seem to have that the mind is something which perceives, and which remains the same throughout our lives. For example, it is obviously true to say that I saw certain things yesterday, and certain other things today. None of the things I perceive now are identical with the things I perceived yesterday. But I am the same person as I was yesterday, it was I and none other who perceived those things. Therefore something, my mind or self, persisted through from yesterday, and it was not a perception. The question is then, what is it that persisted from yesterday to today? Hume's answer to this is that nothing persisted, because if anything did, it must be a perception, and no perceptions persisted. The second question then arises: if there is no independent entity, the mind, which remains identically the same from day to day, what gives us the illusion that there is such an entity? Hume's answer to this is that the illusion is a result of another confusion about the use of the phrase 'the same'. This confusion is not very easy to explain, and Hume himself does not do it at all clearly. Perhaps it can be put like this:[22] when we say 'This is the same box as I saw before', we are not saying anything about the contents of the box. We identify boxes otherwise than by their contents. Furthermore, boxes continue to exist, and remain distinct, even if they are empty. And when we say 'This is the same box', we do not mean that this box is in the same place as the one we saw before. But when we say 'This is the same slag-heap as the one I saw before', we *are* only saying something either about the contents of the heap, or about its spatial position. We do identify slag-heaps by their contents and position. We must remember, though, that when we say 'This is the same slag-heap', we do not necessarily mean that any of the contents are the same, but only that the change of contents has been relatively gradual. And you cannot have a slag-heap with nothing in it: you only have the place where the slag-heap was. Hume's contention is that we confuse identity of slag-heap with identity of boxes, and because a box is something different from and existing independently of its contents, so a slag-heap must be something different from, and existing independently of its contents. And the mind is like a slag-heap, rather than like a box. In other words, we come to think that the mind is something different from, and existing independently of its perceptions, whereas this is really not the case.

Hume's explanation, if this really is what he intends, is weakened by the fact that we seem not to have the slightest inclination to regard a slag-heap as something existing independently of its contents, whereas we do so regard the mind. Perhaps a better analogy would be the grin of the Cheshire cat in *Alice in Wonderland*. We do have some inclination to think of a grin as something other than the features that wear it; otherwise Lewis Carroll's joke would not be a joke. Then Hume's theory is that the mind, or self, is like the grin, and perceptions are like the face that grins.

Now, given that Hume is right in saying that there is no independent entity, the mind, which persists from yesterday to today, and given that he explains satisfactorily how we come by the illusion that there is such an entity, there still remains a third question. This is the question, 'What is it that makes two distinct perceptions constituents of the same mind?' If minds were distinct entities, over and above the perceptions they have, we should presumably have some independent method for identifying minds, and then there would be no problem. But if minds are, as Hume thinks, constituted by their perceptions, we are bound to say what relation between perceptions makes them constitute a mind. It must be a relation which holds between all your perceptions, and between all my perceptions, but not between your perceptions and my perceptions. Hume's attempt to solve this problem consists essentially of the two passages about memory and causal connexion, quoted above.

Let us now reconsider these two passages. First here is the one about memory:[23]

For what is the memory but a faculty, by which we raise up the images of past perceptions? And as an image necessarily resembles its object, must not the frequent placing of these resembling perceptions in the chain of thought, convey the imagination more easily from one link to another, and make the whole seem like the continuance of one object?

The point to notice here, is that this is not an explanation of the nature of the required relation between perceptions, nor is it an explanation why there seems to be such a relation. It is another explanation why we think all our perceptions are related to one object, the mind. Furthermore, it seems to be assumed, for the purpose of this explanation, first that there really is a relation between our perceptions that links them 'in the chain of thought', and second that there is something, the imagination, which is 'conveyed' along the chain. Thus, it does seem as if Hume is in fact presupposing the existence of just the two things he professes to explain away.

The other passage ran as follows:

The true idea of the human mind, is to consider it as a system of different perceptions or different existences, which are linked together by the relation of cause and effect, and mutually produce, destroy, influence, and modify each other.

Here then, the relation between perceptions which makes them perceptions of the same mind, is said to be the relation of cause and effect. That is to say, if two perceptions are related by causality, then it necessarily follows that they are perceptions of the same mind. Consequently, if I have perception A, and you have perception B, and no perceptions are shared, there is no causal connexion between A and B. Now, for Hume, to say A causes B is to say one or other of two things. Either it means A is always followed by B, or it means that given A one always expects B. In the first sense it would seem that there is nothing to prevent a causal connexion between my perceptions and your perceptions. It might well be the case that my perception of A is always followed by your perception of B, but not by my perception of B. It might, of course, be suggested that some kind of contiguity is required, in addition to uniformity of sequence; but this could not be spatial contiguity, since not all perceptions have spatial properties. The only possible kind of contiguity here would be membership of the same mind, and this is the very thing that requires to be explained. Again, to say that the person who perceives A also perceives B *means* that the person who perceives A is bound to expect B, is obviously inadequate. One reason for this is that, if the person who perceives A does expect B, he must have perceived both A and B on some previous occasion, without expecting B.

We conclude, therefore, that Hume's attempt to explain how perceptions are bound together in a single mind is not successful. It is clear from the following quotations that Hume was himself well aware of the difficulties:[24]

Having thus loosen'd all our particular perceptions, when I proceed to explain the principle of connexion, which binds them together, and makes us attribute to them a real simplicity and identity; I am sensible, that my account is very defective, and that nothing but the seeming evidence of the precedent reasonings cou'd have induced me to receive it. If perceptions are distinct existences, they form a whole only by being connected together. But no connexions among distinct existences are ever discoverable by the human understanding. We only *feel* a connexion or determination of the thought, to pass from one object to another.

132

But all my hopes vanish, when I come to explain the principles, that unite our successive perceptions in our thought or consciousness. I cannot discover any theory, which gives me satisfaction on this head.

Did our perceptions either inhere in something simple and individual, or did the mind perceive some real connexion among them, there wou'd be no difficulty in the case. For my part, I must plead the privilege of a sceptic, and confess, that this difficulty is too hard for my understanding.

Hume modestly suggests that perhaps someone else will solve this problem, but in fact his modesty is misplaced. Perception by the same mind cannot be any perceivable relation among perceptions, nor can it be any perceivable relation between these perceptions and some other object. For in either case it would not be self-contradictory to say that we have the perceptions, but the relation does not hold between them. This holds for what Hume would regard as an illusory felt connexion, as well as for a real one. In general, to ascertain whether a certain relation exists between objects, we have to perceive them, and then in addition to this, we have to note the relation between them. But to ascertain whether we perceive two objects, we just have to perceive them, or not, as the case may be. No further observations are necessary. Thus perception cannot be a relation, at least in the ordinary sense. The only possible solution is to say that all existing perceptions are in the same mind, a form of solipsism to which Hume is driven, but which he is naturally unwilling to accept.

It is important to try to disentangle the features of Hume's philosophy which led him to this impasse. It will be remembered that he is trying to define what is meant by the words 'soul', 'mind', 'self', and it will be convenient first to make some remarks on definitions in general. Definitions may be classified, rather roughly, into what I shall call *ostensible* definitions and *functional* definitions. An ostensible definition of a thing is a definition of it in terms of immediately perceivable qualities. A functional definition of a thing is, as its name implies, a definition of the thing in terms of its functions. For example, if we say: The St George's Cross is a red cross on a white ground, then that is an ostensible definition. If we say: A physician is one who cures the sick, then that is a functional definition. An ostensible definition is appropriate when someone asks: What is an X? meaning by this: How can I identify Xs at sight? A functional definition is appropriate when someone asks: What is an X? meaning: What can I expect from Xs if I come across them? It is usually obvious from the nature of the question, or from its context, what sort of definition is called for.

Some sorts of difficulty arise because many objects seem to have both an ostensible and a functional definition. If this were really so, the two definitions would be logically equivalent, and this is impossible, for apparent qualities cannot entail functions, nor can functions entail apparent qualities. Nevertheless, we often do have these twin definitions. For example, we may define the Union Flag as a certain pattern of red, white, and blue. Or we may define the Union Flag as the flag which every British subject is entitled to show on any occasion. It is important to notice that we may use both these definitions as definitions of the Union Flag, and which definition we use will be determined solely by the purpose of our questioner, when he asks: What is the Union Flag? It will depend on whether he wants to know how to identify the flag at sight, or whether he wants to know if he is entitled to show it, and so on. Thus in a modified sense, both definitions are definitions of the Union Flag, and this may incline us to suppose that they are logically equivalent. The inclination is quickly rectified if we consider the matter attentively, but we do not always consider the matter attentively. And there are many other instances which help to confuse us. Another example is the definition of a boot. If someone asks: What is a boot? we may say it is a leather object of certain shape and construction, or we may say it is an object whose function is to protect the foot. It will depend on whether our questioner wants to know how to recognize boots, or whether he wants to know how to make good use of them. In this case there are other features which strengthen the feeling that there is some kind of logical connexion between the apparent qualities of a thing, and its function.[25]

It thus seems that enquiries into the nature, or the definition, of a thing, cannot usually be carried through without considering the purpose for which such information is required. This is particularly important in philosophy where it does often seem that we wish to know the nature of a thing for its own sake, as it were, independently of all other considerations. Indeed, the impractical character of philosophical speculation has been seen by many as one of its chief virtues. We may now suspect that this is not really so, and that in the ordinary processes of philosophical reasoning, the purpose of the question is concealed rather than revealed. This would go some way towards accounting for the very refractory nature of such questions.

Now philosophers, in their attempts to understand the nature of things, often show a decided preference for one particular kind of definition. Some feel that they gain real understanding of a thing, only if they can recognize it at sight, or visualize it clearly. Others feel that real understanding lies in an insight into the function of a thing. Hume and other empiricists are examples of the former tendency; perhaps the ancient Greek philosophers were examples of the latter. The former demand ostensible definitions, the latter functional definitions. Philosophers who feel that they understand the nature of a thing only when they have provided an ostensible definition of it, sometimes find themselves in difficulties. For there are many things which are conceived of primarily or solely in terms of their function, and the objects which fulfil this function may have no apparent qualities in common. For example, food is naturally defined as that which nourishes, and we may search in vain for any apparent qualities common to, and peculiar to, all food. Thus, an ostensible definition, or even an ostensible characterization, of food, is out of the question. The situation is aggravated when a philosopher maintains, as Hume does, that a word has meaning only if its meaning can be explained in terms of apparent qualities, that is, only if an ostensible definition can be given. It would seem that Hume should say that the word 'food' is meaningless.

Of course, Hume does not say that the word 'food' is meaningless, simply because all articles of food do have apparent qualities, even though they have no such qualities in common. The philosophically interesting situation arises only when something is functionally defined, and has no ostensible definition just because it cannot or does not have any apparent qualities whatever. These are the entities which Hume wishes to reject when he argues against occult powers and objects. In doing so he was no doubt attacking a deep-rooted superstition. It is one of the presuppositions of primitive thought that everything that happens is an action performed by an agent, nothing happens of its own accord.[26] Consequently, if there is no visible or tangible agent, there must be an invisible intangible one. Thus the world is crowded with invisible powers, which influence our lives, and which are either beyond our control, or may be controlled by magical and religious practices. This may be contrasted with the scientific view, which also maintains that nothing happens of its own accord, but holds that the agencies are always visible and tangible, although they may sometimes be rather difficult to find.

In philosophy we seem to have the conception of agencies which cannot logically have any apparent qualities, and the empiricist wishes to dispose of these. For example, we form the notion of material substance as that which possesses apparent qualities. The function of material substance is to hold material qualities together as one object, and to provide something for them to belong to. It is obvious from this that material substance cannot have any ostensible definition, and there are no apparent qualities which are qualities of material substance as such. One can, as it were, see the qualities, but not the substance. The doctrine of material substance is rejected by empiricists on the ground that qualities need not be possessed by anything, and need not be held together by anything. The illusion that there must be something performing these functions is a result of confusing the predicative use of the verb 'to be' with a relational term like 'is next to'. This is encouraged by philosophical usage, which is inclined to replace 'A is red' with 'A possesses the quality of redness'. And 'possesses' is certainly a relational term in plain English. It makes it look as if A possesses the redness, just as a man possesses sixpence. And of course if sixpence is possessed, it must be possessed by somebody. But in fact the predicative 'to be' is not a relational verb like 'to possess'.

Now the most natural way of defining the mind or soul is in terms of its functions, and two such definitions are possible. We may say, either that the mind is that which thinks, perceives, and feels, or that the mind is that which controls the movements of the physical body. One of the long-standing problems of philosophy is to explain how one and the same object can perform both these functions. But it was not Hume's problem, for he had no interest in the mind considered as that which controls the movements of the body. His problem was to identify the object which performs the function of perceiving. A difficulty arises, because the relation between the mind and the objects it is said to 'perceive' is very similar to the relation between material substance and the qualities it is said to 'possess'. Material substance must be different from any of the qualities it has, and mind must be different from any of the perceptions it has. Thus it appears that the mind, like material substance, is invoked solely to perform a function, and it then appears that anything which performs this function must, because of the nature of the function, necessarily be invisible and intangible.

The doctrine of the impossibility of unperceivable entities thus leads to the rejection of mind, or mental substance, just as it led to the rejection of material substance. And in precise analogy with the conclusion that particular material objects are nothing but bundles of sensible qualities, we have Hume's conclusion that the mind is nothing but a bundle of perceptions. That is to say, although Hume did not himself give this account of material objects, his account of the nature of minds is exactly parallel with it.[27] Now whatever we may think of the theory that material objects are nothing but bundles of qualities, there are discrepancies which weaken the analogy tacitly drawn by Hume, and which produce an insoluble problem. In the first place, whereas the verb 'to be', used predicatively, is certainly not a transitive or relational verb, the verb 'to perceive' is such a verb. The grammatical properties of 'perceive' are exactly like the grammatical properties of 'possess'. Thus we cannot explain away mental substance as we can material substance, for all transitive verbs really do require two terms. Secondly, because material objects are always located in space, we have a ready explanation of what we mean by a bundle of qualities. We mean a number of qualities which coincide in space. And different bundles are different, in the sense that they are spatially separated. But perceptions are not located in space, so we cannot explain what is meant by a bundle of perceptions in this manner. Consequently, we are given a way of deciding whether two qualities are in the same bundle, but no way of deciding whether two perceptions are in the same bundle.

The difficulty may be summed up in the following argument. First we have the following premisses:

(1) If X is not self-contradictory, then 'I perceive that X' is not self-contradictory.

(2) 'I perceive that X' entails X.

(3) 'I perceive that X and Y' entails 'I perceive that X, and I perceive that Y'.

(4) 'A exists, and I do not perceive A' is not self-contradictory.

(5) 'I perceive that A exists' entails 'I perceive A'.

Now, by (1) and (4) we have:

(6) 'I perceive that A exists, and that I do not perceive A' is not self-contradictory.

138

By (3) and (6),

    (7) 'I perceive that A exists, and I perceive that I do not perceive A' is not self-contradictory.

By (2), (5), and (7),

    (8) 'I perceive A and I do not perceive A' is not self-contradictory.

Since (8) is false, and the argument is formally valid, one or more of the premisses (1) to (5) must be false. It hardly seems possible to question (2), (3), and (5), and if we do not do this, we must conclude that (1) or (4) or both are false. That is to say, either there are cases where X is not self-contradictory and yet 'I perceive that X' is self-contradictory, or else 'A exists, and I do not perceive A' is self-contradictory. The latter of these alternatives makes what I perceive logically coextensive with what exists, and this is the doctrine of psychological solipsism. On the other hand, the principle that if X is not self-contradictory then 'I perceive that X' is not self-contradictory, is one of Hume's most fundamental assumptions. It is the doctrine that what is not self-contradictory is conceivable, and what is conceivable is perceivable. That is the basic postulate of empiricism. It thus appears that Hume must either reject empiricism or accept solipsism. [28] Naturally he does not wish to do either of these things, and he can comfortably ignore the necessity of making a choice, until he comes to deal directly with the nature of the mind.

CHAPTER 7

THE SCEPTICAL PHILOSOPHY

I

WE shall now try to sum up Hume's philosophy, and compare his views with those of some other philosophers. If the summing up consisted simply in the correct application of a classificatory noun our task would be a simple one. Hume professes to be, and is in fact, a *Sceptic*. But such pigeon-holing is of no value whatever unless we have decided exactly what a Sceptic is, and in what sense the term is applicable to Hume.

A Sceptic is often taken to be one who denies the possibility of human knowledge, and this sense has been established philosophical usage for a long time. It is, however, a perversion of the original meaning of the Greek term, which is derived from the verb *skeptesthai*, to look carefully at, to consider. Thus a Sceptic was simply one who inquired or investigated carefully. Our source for classical Scepticism is the work of Sextus Empiricus, who states there are three kinds of philosophy, the Dogmatic, the Academic, and the Sceptic.[1] The Dogmatists claim to have discovered the truth, the Academics say the truth 'cannot be grasped', and the Sceptics 'go on seeking'. The Sceptics had no doctrine, in the ordinary sense, instead they had a 'way of enquiry' and an 'end' which they sought. The end was not any kind of knowledge.

If we are to assess Hume's claim to Scepticism, we must compare his methods and aims with those of the Sceptics themselves. The latter are summed up by Sextus Empiricus as follows:[2]

The origin of Scepticism is the hope of attaining *ataraxia*. Men who were disquieted by the contradictions in things and in doubt as to which alternative they ought to accept, were led on to inquire what is true in things and what false, hoping by the settlement of this question to attain *ataraxia*. The principle of Scepticism is to oppose to every proposition an equal proposition; for we believe that as a consequence of this we end by ceasing to dogmatize.

The Sceptic does not suspend judgement on all matters. On this point he has been widely misunderstood in ancient, as well as in modern times. Sextus makes a distinction as follows:[3]

When we say the Sceptic refrains from dogmatizing we do not use the term 'dogma', as some do, in the broader sense of 'acceptance of a thing' (for the Sceptic acquiesces in the sentiments which are necessary products of immediate experience).

We say he does not dogmatize, using 'dogma' in the sense of 'assent to one of the occult matters of investigation'; for the Pyrrhonean philosopher assents to nothing that is occult.

Two conclusions emerge from these, and other similar passages. First, the Sceptic is particularly concerned to avoid dogmatical opinions on occult or hidden matters, as opposed to those which are objects of sense experience. Such matters, he says, cannot be decided, and our only hope is to arrive at a suspense of judgement, a kind of indifference, about them. Second, the Sceptic does not suspend judgement on matters of immediate sense experience,[4] nor does he attempt to deny those sentiments and beliefs which are the necessary *and involuntary* products of sense experience.

Our investigations have shown quite clearly that Hume's position is very close to this Sceptical view, if not identical with it. Hume, too, says that we cannot ever come to any conclusions about occult matters, and that when we have discovered this we shall sit down quietly and cease to worry about these things. He says that our everyday beliefs are the natural and unreasoned products of our experience. For example:[5]

Belief is the necessary result of placing the mind in such circumstances. It is an operation of the soul, when we are so situated, as unavoidable as to feel the passion of love, when we receive benefits; or hatred, when we meet with injuries. All these operations are a species of natural instincts, which no reasoning or process of the thought and understanding is able either to produce or to prevent.

Tho' we must endeavour to render all our principles as universal as possible, by tracing up our experiments to the utmost, and explaining all effects from the simplest and fewest causes, 'tis still certain we cannot go beyond experience; and any hypothesis, that pretends to discover the ultimate original qualities of human nature, ought at first to be rejected as presumptuous and chimerical.

The only method of freeing learning, at once, from these abstruse questions, is to enquire seriously into the nature of the human understanding, and show, from an exact analysis of its powers and capacity, that it is by no means fitted for such remote and abstruse subjects. We must submit to this fatigue, in order to live at ease ever after.

We must now try to decide exactly what are these occult matters, these remote and abstruse subjects, against which both Hume and the Sceptics direct their attacks.

The Stoics believed that some things are manifest or obvious, and some are hidden or occult. An example of something manifest is the fact that it is now day-time, or night-time, as the case may be. There are three kinds of hidden things:[6] (1) Things altogether hidden because, as a fact, they are beyond our grasp, as for example is the number of the stars; (2) Things sometimes hidden, as events in London are hidden from one in Brighton; (3) Things hidden by nature or things not of such a kind as to be perceived, perhaps a gravitational field would be an example of such an entity, or the luminiferous ether. The manifest things are known directly, things altogether hidden are not known at all. Things sometimes hidden, and things hidden by nature are known by signs, the former by *suggestive* signs, and the latter by *indicative* signs. The suggestive sign is defined as follows:

A sign is suggestive when, being mentally associated with the thing signified, it by its clearness at the time of its perception, though the thing signified remains hidden, suggests to us the thing associated with it, which is not clearly perceived at the moment as for instance in the case of smoke and fire.

The association, we are told, is the product of past experience.[7] Let us compare this with one of Hume's definitions of cause:

A cause is an object precedent and contiguous to another, and so united with it, that the idea of the one determines the mind to form

142

the idea of the other, and the impression of the one to form a more lively idea of the other.

In Hume's case also the union of ideas is the product of past experience. The Sceptics reject the possibility of an indicative sign, that is of a sign which in some quasi-logical sense necessitates the presence of the thing signified. Or rather, they suspend judgement on the possibility of such signs. In a like manner, Hume argues against the possibility of a necessary connexion between cause and effect. In these respects, then, there is some parallel between Hume's views and those of the Sceptics.

The essential feature of Scepticism is that it presents, not a doctrine, but a *technique* for suspending judgement on certain matters of enquiry. This technique consists chiefly of eliciting the fact that there is no logical connexion between the way in which we arrive at a belief and the truth of that belief. Even if all the beliefs arrived at by a certain method *are* true, there is no necessity about this, they could have been false. Thus the possibility of knowledge is denied in just this sense: If by 'knowledge' you mean a belief arrived at by a logically infallible method, then there is no knowledge. That is Scepticism. The Sceptic does not deny that some ways of arriving at beliefs are better than others, in the sense of yielding more true beliefs, or being as a fact more reliable. He does not say we should trust to instinct, or wishful thinking, rather than our natural powers of calculation. He does not recommend that we should suspend judgement on all matters, both theoretical and practical. All he says is that no method we use, not even when we employ our peculiarly human powers of reflective thought and logical calculation, issues infallibly in true beliefs. And he recommends that we should remember this. Hume's final position on these matters is not distinguishable from that of classical Scepticism.[8]

Now there seems to be a certain possible inconsistency in the Sceptical view. The recognition that no method of inquiry yields infallible results is supposed to produce a suspense of judgement on some matters, but not on others. In practical affairs, at any rate, the fact that no methods we can use are infallible does not, and should not, prevent us from using those methods and placing our trust in the results. In ordinary life we expect to make some mistakes, and indeed we could hardly live at all if we demanded absolute security in every contingency. Often enough the urgency of making some decision overbalances the importance of deciding which is the right decision to make. But it is abundantly clear that the main objects of Scepticism are not practical affairs, but some other matters. Furthermore, the peculiar feature of these other matters must be that, if any decision is to be made about them at all, it must be an absolutely secure and infallible decision, and failing this it is better to suspend judgement altogether, rather than run any risk of making a mistake. They must therefore be matters of enormous importance, although they do not appear to be of very great urgency.

We are also told that *ataraxia*, which is the aim of the Sceptic, is 'an untroubled and tranquil condition of the soul', and this aim is to be attained, not by answering the questions that trouble us, but by suspending judgement and ceasing to dogmatize.[9] The Sceptic tries to produce this suspense of judgement by a process of *opposition*, which consists in countering any dogmatic assertion with another assertion. For example, if someone argues the existence of Providence from the order of the universe, the Sceptic opposes to this the fact that often the good fare ill and the bad fare well, which suggests that Providence does not exist.

Now when Hume is stating his philosophical aims, the following sentences occur, among others:[10]

When we see, that we have arrived at the utmost extent of human reason, we sit down contented, tho' we be perfectly satisfied in the main of our ignorance.

And as this impossibility of making any farther progress is enough to satisfy the reader, so the writer may derive a more delicate satisfaction from the free confession of his ignorance, and from his prudence in avoiding that error, into which so many have fallen, of imposing their conjectures and hypotheses on the world for the most certain principles. When this mutual contentment and satisfaction can be obtained betwixt the master and scholar, I know not what more we can require of our philosophy.

Hume too was against dogmatism and for suspense of judgement, and he thought the latter issued in a kind of contentment. Thus far he was a Sceptic. But we must observe that the method he proposed for producing this suspense of judgement differs from that proposed by the Sceptics. The Sceptics have a way of counterbalancing arguments, whereas Hume tries to define the limits of human knowledge. In this sense Hume was not a Sceptic, for he did have a dogma, namely that the human understanding has such and such limits.

Hume and the Sceptics tell us in effect that we can know only what seems to be so, and never what is really so. They apply this at first to matters of fact. For example, we may know that honey seems sweet to us, but not that it really is sweet. We are, as it were, bound to appearances and separated for ever from the real nature of things. Again, we cannot know the future, because the expectations we form, and our methods of forming them, are both perfectly compatible with subsequent disappointment. The epistemological doubt invariably turns on the theoretical fallibility of our methods, and never on their failure in practice. There is a simple reason for this: our methods are successful in practice, and if they were not we should either abandon them or perish. But the theoretical fallibility of our methods of inquiry provides no reason for abandoning them, because this feature appears to be common to all the methods which may be open to us. The aim both of Hume and of the Sceptics is to assure us of this, and to make us content with what we have. All this applies to things which are sometimes hidden, and where error may have serious practical consequences.

The things hidden by nature are said by the Sceptics to be altogether unknowable, and by Hume to be not only unknowable but even inconceivable. These are the matters concerning which we are advised to practise indifference. Our usual methods of investigation, since they make essential use of sense-experience, are here incompetent, since there is no way of ascertaining whether they are successful or not. The example so often given is that of the essential or real nature of things, as opposed to their apparent nature which is revealed by sense-experience. We need not here consider how it was that philosophers came to think things had a real nature not revealed in sense-experience. No solid and satisfactory explanation of this has yet been given.[11] All we need to notice is that, if everyday experience has no bearing whatever on the real nature of things, then the question as to the real nature of things is of no importance whatever in everyday life. Inquiry into the real nature of things seems entirely purposeless: it is impossible to say what we should do with such knowledge if we had it. Consequently, it is at least very hard to see why our ignorance on this point should produce a state of turbulence in the soul, a state which it is the business of philosophy to mollify. Dogmatists and Sceptics alike agree that the purpose of philosophy is to tranquillize the soul, and we see that, according to Hume, this is one of the effects of philosophy, even if it is not its principal purpose. It may, of course be contended that the motive for philosophy is the satisfaction of a disinterested curiosity, but however this may be in some cases, there is no doubt that for most philosophers there has been some other motive. For most of them there is some powerful and obscure hope or fear at the heart of philosophy, and this has no direct connexion with a disinterested curiosity concerning the nature of things.[12]

The true function of Scepticism becomes clearer if we consider the kinds of philosophy which were the objects of Sceptical attack. The common feature of these systems was that they believed Ethics to be the chief part of philosophy, and epistemology and ontology were important only so far as they bore upon ethical problems. Indeed, Ethics was something more than the chief part of philosophy, it was called the 'crown' and the 'soul' of the subject, the implication being that all other parts derived their entire importance and vitality from their connexion with Ethics.[13] Such a conception is natural enough, if it is supposed that philosophy has to

do with the conduct of life and with the attainment of a state
of personal blessedness, and if it is further supposed that in
this connexion moral considerations necessarily outweigh
any other possible combination of considerations. And it is
common belief, even at the present time, that moral considerations, where they apply, are of ultimate and overwhelming importance. Thus, if a certain course of action is
morally right, this is felt to be a decisive recommendation, no
matter what other arguments may be brought against it.
Likewise, if it is morally wrong, this consideration overcomes
the weightiest reasons of expediency which may be brought
in favour of its performance. The consequences of moral success or failure also are commonly felt to be vast, imponder-
able, and in some measure obscure. Viewed in this way then,
it does seem that in Ethics we have sufficient cause for that
profound disquietude and turbulence of soul, of which the
Sceptics speak, and which it is their purpose to eliminate.

The Sceptics believed that a kind of irrational dread resulted from the opinion that things are by nature good or
evil,[14] and they accordingly aimed at the abandonment of
this opinion. There is some possibility of misunderstanding
here. The Sceptics did not deny the existence of moral feelings, not did they suggest that such feelings do not play an
important part in human affairs. They did not suggest that
what we commonly call moral considerations do not or
should not affect our decisions. What they did mean to suggest was that there is no kind of consideration governing
conduct which has that enormous and quite peculiar importance which is so often associated with what are commonly called moral considerations. The Sceptics thought
that the idea that things are by nature good or evil resulted in,
or perhaps merely reflected, the attachment of an *excessive*
weight to matters of morality. The general character of the
idea they were attacking may be conjectured with some
assurance. It was the idea that moral decisions have a *supernatural* importance, and are in this way distinguished from
ordinary non-moral decisions. Our everyday decisions affect
our future happiness and our relationships with our fellow

men in this life, but moral decisions affect our happiness to all eternity, even after we have left this world, and they affect our relationships with invisible, supernatural beings. What is more, the whole of our eternal future is fixed and determined by our conduct in this life: we have no chance of correcting ourselves on receiving enlightenment after death.

It is obvious enough that anyone who seriously believes such things as this will be led to ascribe a quite overwhelming importance to any question he has been taught to designate as 'moral', no matter how trivial or even ridiculous that particular question might seem to others who do not share his beliefs. And matters of the greatest practical importance will dwindle to nothing, for such a person, if he does not happen to attach to them the magic word. It is also plain to see that, if someone seriously believes that moral failure results inevitably in eternal damnation and the unappeasable wrath of God, then any kind of doubt concerning moral decisions will produce in him the greatest anxiety and confusion of soul. He will, to put it bluntly and colloquially, be terrified out of his wits.[15]

Now there are only two sources to which a man can turn for answers to questions: he can either place his trust in some authority, or he can seek for himself. And trust in an authority is either a matter of upbringing and not a matter of choice, or it is a matter of choice and the seeker is once more thrown back on his own decision. In the ordinary affairs of life our instructor is experience. We expect to make some mistakes and to profit by them. Or if we trust some authority, we trust him because he has already learned by experience, and the correctness of his teaching can be assessed by its results. We can learn from experience what things give us pleasure or pain, and also what things excite the praise or indignation of our fellow men. Thus there is no difficulty in determining moral conduct in any such sense. But if moral conduct is conceived as conduct attended with supernatural sanctions a very serious difficulty at once arises. It is clear that if our present conduct has inevitable, interminable, and terrible

148

consequences in an after-life, this is easily the most important factor in any decisions we may now make. On the other hand, it is from the nature of the case impossible to learn from experience what kinds of conduct have these consequences until it is too late to correct ourselves. Present experience is silent concerning events beyond the grave. Thus if moral conduct is so conceived, it follows both that moral decisions are the only decisions of any real importance, and that experience provides no basis whatever for making such decisions.

The quest for ataraxy or tranquillity of soul, as a cure for moral and superstitious over-anxiety, was the common pursuit of philosophers in later antiquity. Three solutions were provided. The Stoics accepted this overburdening of moral decisions, but claimed we can have moral knowledge, and that this is to be obtained by a following a special philosophical discipline. They also softened and refined the crude and harsh eschatology of the common folk. The Epicureans said there is no life after death, and the gods have no interest in men and their doings. Morality for them consisted of the acquisition of happiness in this life, and in amiable social intercourse. The Sceptics claimed that eschatological knowledge is impossible, and that peace of mind follows naturally upon appreciation of this fact.

Anyone who tries to assess the nature and purpose of Hume's philosophical investigations is faced with certain difficulties. In the first place, there is a considerable difference in attitude between his two chief works, the *Treatise* and the *Enquiries*. Secondly, we have little information about Hume's early development, before he wrote the *Treatise*.[16] We must try to explain the former, and make the best of the latter. Three points emerge fairly clearly. First, Hume himself regarded the *Enquiries* as the definitive statement of his philosophical views, and this was his considered opinion. Second, the purpose of the *Enquiries* is more consciously and assuredly sceptical than the *Treatise*. Third, there are convincing arguments to show that Hume's primary interest was in Moral Philosophy.

In support of the first of these statements, we may observe that Hume produced no serious philosophical writings after the *Enquiries*, and that an advertisement is prefaced to the second edition of the *Enquiries*, recording the author's desire 'that the following Pieces may alone be regarded as containing his philosophical sentiments and principles'. The calm and resolved scepticism of the *Enquiry concerning the Human Understanding* contrasts strongly with the knotted argumentation and progressively increasing stresses of the first Book of the *Treatise of Human Nature*. We need only compare the triumphant conclusion of the former with the anxious and apologetic ending of the latter. The last words of the *Enquiry* are a final rejection of metaphysics:[17]

If we take in our hand any volume; of divinity or school metaphysics, for instance; let us ask, Does it contain any abstract reasoning concerning quantity or number? No. Does it contain any experimental reasoning concerning matter of fact and existence? No. Commit it then to the flames: for it can contain nothing but sophistry and illusion.

Towards the end of Book I of the *Treatise* he says:

Where am I, or what? From what causes do I derive my existence, and to what condition shall I return? Whose favour shall I court, and whose anger must I dread? What beings surround me? and on whom have I any influence, or who have any influence on me? I am confounded with all these questions, and begin to fancy myself in the most deplorable condition imaginable, inviron'd with the deepest darkness, and utterly depriv'd of the use of every member and faculty.

If the questions asked here were intended in their ordinary matter-of-fact sense, the answers would be obvious enough, and there would be no cause either for confusion or for deplorable imaginings. Evidently they are metaphysical questions, both in the sense that they are not amenable to the usual processes of rational enquiry, and in the sense that they are of the greatest importance in determining our course of conduct. Now Hume already had at his disposal all the reasons for saying that metaphysical questions cannot be decided, that discussion of them must 'contain nothing but sophistry and illusion', that they must be meaningless questions, and that therefore they cannot be of the slightest importance in the determination of conduct or in any other connexion. In the *Treatise* he seems to recognize all this. But they are not the things which in the end lead him to reject mataphysical speculation and free himself of 'the pensive melancholy which it induces'. The sequel to the above passage runs as follows: [18]

> Most fortunately it happens, that since reason is incapable of dispelling these clouds, nature herself suffices to that purpose, and cures me of this philosophical melancholy and delirium, either by relaxing this bent of mind, or by some avocation, and lively impression of my senses, which obliterate all these chimeras. I dine, I play a game of backgammon, I converse, and am merry with my friends; and when after three or four hours' amusement, I wou'd return to these speculations, they appear so cold, and strain'd, and ridiculous, that I cannot find in my heart to enter into them any further.

Thus his relief from philosophical questioning comes, not simply from the recognition that such questions are meaningless, but from an involuntary, and seemingly independent change of mood. The ancient Sceptics made similar observations: [19]

> So, too, the Sceptics were in hopes of gaining tranquillity by means of a decision regarding the disparity of the objects of sense and of thought, and being unable to effect this they suspended judgement; and then found that tranquillity, as if by chance, followed upon their suspense, even as a shadow follows its substance.

> And they compare themselves with the painter who, impatient at failing to achieve some effect, threw his sponge at the canvas in disgust, and the mark of the sponge produced just the effect he desired.

Hume and the Sceptics, then, had good cause to associate philosophy with superstition. Certain philosophical questions are said by Hume to induce 'melancholy and delirium', euphemisms, we may suppose, for fear. Superstitious doubts and beliefs are primarily associated with fear. These philosophical questions cannot be decided by the usual means of rational inquiry, namely observation and deduction. Superstitious beliefs are certainly not arrived at by rational inquiry, and although some of them may be tested against experience, it is a well-known fact that such tests, even when negative, have little or no effect, and are somehow discounted by superstitious persons. Superstitious doubts and fears are somehow immune to experience, and they lose their power, not by the accumulation of evidence, but when they cease to have that kind of immunity. Thus the resolution of superstitious doubt closely resembles the Sceptic account of the resolution of metaphysical doubt.

Philosophy and superstition are connected with religion. Hume says that superstition is a species of false religion. By this he appears to mean that one kind of religion derives its strength and influence from the exploitation and intensification of those irrational fears to which men are naturally subject in certain circumstances. False religions of this kind often use bad philosophy to give a semblance of rationality to their absurd principles. According to Hume the Roman Catholic religion falls in this class. The other species of false religion is *enthusiasm*, and by this Hume means the belief that one is inspired by God. Such a belief is not attended with exaggerated superstitious fears, but it is attended with an equally exaggerated complacency and elevation of the spirits. It is, so to speak, an over-compensation. Enthusiasm is not a characteristic feature of the organized religions, but it lies at the root of one kind of philosophy. Many philosophers have believed their aim to be the attainment of a specially close relation, amounting even to identity, with a Divine Being.

II

Some further light can be thrown on Hume's philosophical views by comparing them with those of John Locke(1621–1704) and George Berkeley (1685–1753). It was Locke who first directed attention to the limited nature of the human mind. In a preface to his chief work (which was significantly entitled *An Essay concerning the Human Understanding*) he makes the following observation:[20]

Were it fit to trouble thee with the history of this Essay, I should tell thee, that five or six friends meeting at my chamber, and discoursing on a subject very remote from this, found themselves quickly at a stand, by the difficulties that rose on every side. After we had awhile puzzled ourselves, without coming any nearer a resolution of those doubts which perplexed us, it came into my thoughts that we took a wrong course; and that before we set ourselves upon inquiries of that nature, it was necessary to examine our own abilities, and see what *objects* our understandings were, or were not, fitted to deal with.

The subject of the discussion appears to have been the principles of natural religion. A little later on he says:

Till that was done I suspected we began at the wrong end, and in vain sought for satisfaction in a quiet and sure possession of truths that most concerned us, whilst we let loose our thoughts into the vast ocean of Being; as if all that boundless extent were the natural and undoubted possession of our understandings, wherein there was nothing exempt from its decisions, or that escaped its comprehension. Thus men, extending their enquiries beyond their capacities, and letting their thoughts wander into those depths where they can find no sure footing, it is no wonder that they raise questions and multiply disputes, which, never coming to any clear resolution, are proper only to continue and increase their doubts, and to confirm them at last in perfect scepticism.

Locke concludes that the human mind is limited, and that 'the comprehension of our understandings comes exceeding short of the vast extent of things', but he thinks that when we properly appreciate our limitations we shall be perfectly content, because we shall then see that we have all the knowledge we can possibly need or make use of. This accurate adjustment of human intellectual powers to human needs, Locke piously ascribes to 'the bountiful Author of our being'. He describes human needs as follows:[21]

Our business here is not to know all things, but those which concern our conduct. If we can find out those measures, whereby a rational creature, put in that state in which man is in in this world, may and ought to govern his opinions, and actions depending thereon, we need not to be troubled that some other things escape our knowledge.

Locke's delimitation of the scope of human inquiry is, like Hume's, founded upon the sensualistic theory of ideas, but his conclusions differ in several respects from Hume's. He suspects what Hume proves, namely that 'natural philosophy is not capable of being made a science'.[22] By this he means that natural philosophy (what we should call 'science') cannot be made into a deductive discipline like pure mathematics. Thus, the value of natural philosophy, or the experimental investigation of the physical world, does not lie in providing us with knowledge of the ultimate constitution of that world. Its justification cannot be simply intellectual satisfaction. The value of natural philosophy lies in its practical applications, the provision of recipes for making iron and other useful things. Locke would, no doubt, have regarded even modern physics as a kind of superior cookery. And it is not necessary that recipes should embody profound and infallible insights into the nature of the universe, it is necessary only that they should work. For Locke, technology is the only justification for natural philosophy.

Locke differed very much from Hume on moral and religious matters, and it is these he is really thinking of when he says 'Our business here is not to know all things, but those which concern our conduct.' After having recorded his attitude to natural philosophy, he proceeds :[23]

From whence it is obvious to conclude, that, since our faculties are not fitted to penetrate into the internal fabric and real essence of bodies; but yet plainly discover to us the being of a God, and and the knowledge of ourselves, enough to lead us into a full and clear discovery of our duty and great concernment; it will become us, as rational creatures, to employ those faculties we have about what they are most adapted to, and follow the direction of nature, where it seems to point us out the way. For it is rational to conclude that our proper employment lies in those inquiries, and in that sort of knowledge which is most suited to our natural capacities, and carries in it our greatest interest, i.e. the condition of our eternal estate. Hence I think I may conclude, that *morality* is *the proper science and business of mankind in general.*

The principles of natural philosophy, the pronouncements of natural science, may be regarded as 'but very doubtful conjectures', without causing any serious concern or anxiety, but not so the moral law. And this is because mistakes in natural philosophy can at most issue in physical disaster, whereas mistakes in morals may affect 'the condition of our eternal estate'. Therefore, since God has provided man with the means to all the knowledge he needs, God must have provided man with the means to moral knowledge. The only sources of knowledge admitted by Locke are divine revelation and the deductive method proceeding from insights into the relation between ideas. Locke mistrusts divine revelation, and obviously thinks that, if it occurs at all, it is very uncommon. And we cannot have real knowledge of another person's divine revelation. Consequently morals must be a science in the seventeenth-century sense of the word, that is to say it must be a deductive discipline.

Although Locke nowhere attempts a full and detailed discussion of moral questions, it is clear that the conclusion that morals must be a deductive discipline is, for him, of the greatest importance. And in this fundamental respect he is much closer to rationalism than to scepticism. His proof of the existence of God follows Descartes, and is worth examination on account of its fallacious character.[24] He differs from Descartes in maintaining that we have no innate idea of God, or rather that our idea of God must be derived from experience. He argues as follows:

(1) I exist (i.e. he, Locke, exists).
(2) Everything that exists must either (*a*) have always existed, or (*b*) have been produced by something else which existed before it.
(3) I have not always existed.

He concludes from the first two of these propositions that:

(4) Something has always existed.

155

Now (4) is ambiguous. Locke interprets it as meaning that there must be *some one thing* which has always existed, and he proceeds to identify this supposed eternally existing entity with God. But in this sense (4) does not follow from (1) and (2). If (4) is to be a valid conclusion, it can only mean that at every time in the past, there has been something in existence (but possibly not the same thing all the time). Thus, since the existence of God requires the eternal existence of one particular thing, and this does not follow from the premisses, the proof is formally invalid. Hume would, of course, also criticize the alleged proof on the ground that premiss (2) is not self-evident, and may well be false. Thus, although Locke and Hume have a common starting point in the sensualist theory of ideas, they differ completely on the central philosophical issues, morals and religion.

In Berkeley we find an attitude which neither Locke nor Hume would have found altogether congenial. Berkeley announces that his *Principles of Human Knowledge* are addressed 'particularly to those who are tainted with scepticism, or want a demonstration of the existence and immateriality of God, or the natural immortality of the soul'.[25] He notes, as do Locke and Hume, the seemingly insuperable difficulties in philosophical speculation, but he is not inclined to attribute these to the inadequacy of the human mind faced with problems beyond its powers. 'We should', he says, 'believe that God had dealt more bountifully with the sons of men, than to give them a strong desire for that knowledge which he had placed quite out of their reach.'[26] The difficulties in philosophy are not, according to Berkeley, due either to the intricacy of the subject or to the limitations of the human understanding, but they are due entirely to the perversity of philosophers, who insist on using their reasoning powers in the wrong way. Our vision of the truth is, as it were, obscured by dust clouds which we make ourselves, and the implication is that all we need to do in philosophy is clear away these clouds. The aim of philosophy for Berkeley is clarification.

Berkeley believes that the chief obstacle in the way of philosophical clear-sightedness is 'the opinion that the mind hath a power of framing *abstract ideas*'.[27] We need not bother here either with the exact nature of this opinion, or with Berkeley's attack on it, except to note that the chief weapon of his attack is a very literal application of the picture theory of meaning, derived in turn from the sensualist theory of ideas. But the important consequence he draws is that our first care in philosophy must be 'to clear the first principles of knowledge, from the embarrass and delusion of words'. Now although Berkeley uses the theory of ideas and the picture theory of meaning in his attack on abstract ideas, this is not the theory of meaning he adopts in general, for its rigorous and universal application would have resulted in the excision of entities which he wished to maintain. These were human souls, 'spirits', and God. He says that, although we have no idea of the soul, and could not have, yet the word 'soul' is meaningful because some sentences in which this word occurs are meaningful. We have, he says, a *notion* of the soul.[28]

Berkeley maintains that only God, souls or minds, and ideas exist. Here 'idea' is used to cover Hume's 'impressions'. Unlike Hume, he believes that ideas cannot exist by themselves, whereas God and minds can. Thus Berkeley's ontology takes quite another direction, for him souls are substances, and ideas are not substances, in the philosophical sense, where the test of substance is its capacity for independent existence.

On the basis of these remarks we may now compare Berkeley with Hume on the central topic of knowledge, its scope, nature, and purposes. First we observe that Berkeley takes every opportunity to oppose the view, held in common by Locke and Hume, that the human understanding is narrow and limited. Second, he agrees that the experimental method does not and cannot be made to supply any inside knowledge of the workings of nature. But he makes it clear that this is so, not because such knowledge is beyond our grasp, but because there are no inner workings of nature.[29] In this respect he is followed by Hume. Thus, for Berkeley, as for Locke, a justification for natural science is its practical utility, but there is something which Berkeley evidently considers to be much more important:[30]

In perusing the volume of nature it seems beneath the dignity of the human mind to affect an exactness in reducing *each particular phenomenon to general rules*, or showing how it follows from them. We should propose to ourselves nobler views, such as (1) to recreate and exalt the mind, with a prospect of the beauty, *order*, extent, and variety of natural things: hence, by proper inferences, (2) to enlarge our notions of the grandeur, wisdom, and beneficence of the Creator: and lastly (3) to make the several parts of creation, so far as in us lies, subservient to the ends they were designed for, God's glory, and the sustenation and comfort of ourselves and fellow-creatures.

The steady, consistent methods of nature may not unfitly be styled the language of its Author, by which he discovers his attributes to our view, and directs us how to act for the convenience and felicity of life. And to me, those men who frame general rules from the *phenomena*, and afterwards derive the *phenomena* from those rules, seem to be grammarians, and their art the grammar of nature. (Two ways there are of learning a language, either by *rule* or by *practice*.) A man may be well read in the language of nature, without understanding the grammar of it, or being able to say by what rule a thing is so or so.

Thus Berkeley is no uncritical admirer of empirical science. The laws of nature are the grammar of the language of God, but the message conveyed in that language is incomparably more important than any rules of grammar. It is this message which Berkeley thinks is obscured by the philosophical pseudo-concepts, abstract ideas and material substance. He never tells us exactly what God's message is, perhaps he cannot, each of us must read it for himself in the face of nature.

Although Berkeley says the main design of his work is to promote 'the consideration of God, and our *duty*', he has little to say about moral questions. It is plain that he is in no condition of moral doubt or stress: he accepts the Christian ethic with unquestioning simplicity. The 'great truths' which terminate his study of the principles of human knowledge, are nothing more nor less than those taught in every Christian nursery or kindergarten:[31]

> That 'the eyes of the Lord are in every place beholding the evil and the good'; that he is with us and keepeth us in all places whither we go, and giveth us bread to eat, and raiment to put on; that he is present and conscious to our innermost thoughts; and that we have a most absolute and immediate dependence on him.

The moral Berkeley draws is also that of the nursery:

> A clear view of which great truths cannot choose but fill our heart with an awful circumspection and holy fear, which is the strongest incentive to *virtue*, and the best guard against *vice*.

And he concludes that 'having shown the falseness or vanity of those barren speculations, which make the chief employment of learned men', we shall be better disposed to 'reverence and embrace the salutary truths of the gospel'.

The fact that we cannot know the immutability of empirically derived natural laws was not considered by Berkeley to be a serious defect. Far more important for him was our knowledge of religious and moral truths, which he supposed to be evident to us as soon as we had cleared from our eyes the dust of philosophical speculation. The tools forged by Berkeley were used by Hume also to attain a clear vision of things. But whereas Berkeley saw the glory of God, Hume saw nothing but the weakness and vanity of man. So it is that two philosophers may take similar paths, and even so their final reports are utterly at variance.

NOTES

TU: *A Treatise of Human Nature*, Book 1, *Of the Understanding*.
TP: *A Treatise of Human Nature*, Book 2, *Of the Passions*.
TM: *A Treatise of Human Nature*, Book 3, *Of Morals*.

References to the above are by part, section, and paragraph. Thus, TU 2. 5. 1: TU, Part 2, Section 5, Paragraph 1.

ECU: *An Enquiry concerning Human Understanding*.
EPM: *An Enquiry concerning the Principles of Morals*.

References to these are by section, part (where applicable), and paragraph.

DNR: *Dialogues concerning Natural Religion*.

References by part and paragraph.

Other abbreviations used in connexion with the Essays and other minor works are self-explanatory.

WORKS NOT BY HUME

Burton, *Life*: *Life of David Hume*, by T.H.Burton.
Mossner, *Life*: *Life of David Hume*, by A.Mossner.
Locke, *Essay*: *An Essay concerning Human Understanding*, by John Locke.
Berkeley, PHK: *Principles of Human Knowledge*, by George Berkelev.
Sextus, OP: *Outlines of Pyrrhonism*, by Sextus Empiricus.

Other works are quoted in full.

CHAPTER I

1. The material for this section is taken from Burton, and Mossner.
2. Green wrote a very long critical introduction to his edition of Hume, which is made valueless by his complete lack of understanding and sympathy for his subject. His notion of Hume is neatly summed up in the closing sentences of his introduction:

> Our business, however, has not been to moralize, but to show that the philosophy based on the abstraction of feeling, in regard to morals no less than to nature, was with Hume played out, and that the next step forward in speculation could only be an effort to rethink the process of nature and human action from its true beginning

in thought. If this object has been in any way attained, so that the attention of Englishmen 'under five-and-twenty' may be diverted from the anachronistic systems hitherto prevalent among us to the study of Kant and Hegel, an irksome labour will not have been in vain.

3. In the introduction to his edition of the *Enquiries*.

4. N. Kemp Smith, *Philosophy of David Hume*. This is probably still the best full treatment of Hume.

CHAPTER 2

1. The quotations in this and the following paragraphs are taken from TU Introduction.

2.   Here indeed lies the justest and most plausible objection against a considerable part of metaphysics, that they are not properly a science; but arise either from the fruitless efforts of human vanity, which would penetrate into subjects utterly inaccessible to the human understanding, or from the craft of popular superstitions, which, being unable to defend themselves on fair ground, raise these intangling brambles to cover and protect their weakness. Chased from the open country, these robbers fly into the forest, and lie in wait to break in upon every unguarded avenue of the mind, and overwhelm it with religious fears and prejudices. (ECU I. 11.)

The mind of man is subject to certain unaccountable terrors and apprehensions, proceeding either from the unhappy situation of private and public affairs, from ill health, from a gloomy and melancholy disposition, or from the concurrence of all these circumstances. In such a state of mind, infinite unknown evils are dreaded from unknown agents; and where real objects of terror are wanting, the soul, active to its own prejudice, and fostering its predominant inclination, finds imaginary ones, to whose power and malevolence it sets no limits. (*Essays* I. 10.)

One of the most striking features of Hume's ontology is his systematic elimination of 'unknown agents'.

3. The notion of 'contemplative wisdom' as the highest end for man was first clearly formulated by Plato, and he describes a method of Dialectic for achieving this end. It was something more than the satisfaction of simple curiosity. All the metaphysical rituals described in later European philosophy are derived ultimately from Plato's dialectic. The pale ghost of Plato's ideal still haunts the academic mind.

Spinoza is probably the clearest and most uncompromising modern example of the tendencies described in this paragraph.

4. TP 3. 2. 2; 3. 3. 4; T Introduction 9; ECU 4. 1. 12; 5. 1. 1.

5. This was achieved by Albertus Magnus (1193-1280) and Thomas Aquinas (1225-74). Their doctrines remain to the present time the official doctrine of the Roman Catholic Church. For further information see F. C. Copleston, *History of Philosophy*.

6. TU 2. 6. 7; ECU 2.

7. TU 2. 5. 1; 2. 5. 27; 3. 8. 15; 3. 14. 22; 4. 6. 4.

8. TU 4. 2. 30; 3. 14. 25; 4. 6. 6.

Thus we feign the continu'd existence of the perceptions of our senses . . . our propension to confound identity with relation is so great, that we are apt to imagine something unknown and mysterious.

9. This may be contrasted with the usage theory of meaning, in which the meaning of a word is not something that determines the use, it *is* the use.

<h2 style="text-align:center">CHAPTER 3</h2>

1. TU 2. 6. 7.

2. TU 1. 1. 1.

3. TU 1. 1. 3.

4. TU 1. 1. 3.

5. TU 1. 1. 4. The distinction follows Locke, *Essay* 2. 2.

6. TU 1. 2. 1. The distinction here is different from that of Locke, *Essay* 2. 6. For Locke the ideas of reflection are the ideas of thinking and willing, rather than the passions.

7. TU 1. 1. 5; 1. 1. 7.

8. TU 1. 1. 5-9; ECU 2. 5-7.

Hume produces two other observations in this connexion: (1) People lacking in some faculty, such as sight, since birth, are unable to form the ideas appropriate to that faculty; (2) If a man has seen all the shades of some particular colour, with one single exception, then he *can* form the idea of this missing shade, without having experienced it. The first observation is an empirical one and, if correct, supports Hume's theory. The second, if correct, would appear to refute his theory. Hume himself admits that the second observation is contrary to his theory, but does not regard as sufficiently important to warrant serious discussion. For him it is 'the exception that proves the rule'. It is not obvious to the present writer that a man could form the idea (that is to say, a precise visual image) of a shade of blue he had never seen, no matter how many other shades of blue he *had* seen. The question whether persons blind from birth can form visual images may have been investigated by psychologists. If it has, their findings are unknown to the present writer. It is a common fault in philosophical discussion to take for granted factual contentions which seem very plausible, but which really require very careful and difficult investigations to substantiate them.

9. TU 2. 5. 28; 3. 14. 11.
10. TU 1. 1. 1; ECU 2. 1.

In ECU Hume implies that in states of mental disorder ideas may sometimes be as strong and forcible as impressions, and this suggests he thinks the real difference is that impressions have some sort of objective reference, whereas ideas do not. But all this is entirely contrary to his reasonings throughout the remainder of his work.

Hume seems to take it for granted, indeed a matter of obvious definition, that 'the liveliest thought is still inferior to the dullest sensation'. Not everyone would admit the justice of this. Blake said that a person who did not imagine better than he perceived 'could not be said to imagine at all'. There is always the possibility that philosophers' theories are influenced by their aesthetic limitations.

11. TU 1. 3.1–3.
12. TU 2. 6. 4. 'The idea of existence, then, is the very same with the idea of what we conceive to be existent.'
13. The best known statement of the ontological argument is that of Anselm of Canterbury (1033–1109), in his *Proslogium*. It was restated by many philosophers, notably Descartes. It has been attacked by Hume, Kant, and in more recent times Lord Russell, on the ground that 'existence is not a predicate'. See, e.g., Windelband, *History of Philosophy*.
14. ECU 5. 2. 3.
15. TU 2. 6. 7; 4. 2. 7; 4. 2. 15.
16. Berkeley, PHK 23–4; 4; First Dialogue.
17. TU 2. 6. 7.
18. TU 1. 4; ECU 5. 2.
19. TU 3. 8; ECU 5. 2.
20. TU 1. 5. 1.

CHAPTER 4

1. For further information on seventeenth-century science, see, for example, A. Wolf, *A History of Science, Technology and Philosophy in the 16th and 17th Centuries*; Sarton, *History of Science*.

2. The philosophical conception of perfect knowledge appears to be a development from the religious conception of divine inspiration. Pythagoras was very likely the first philosopher to connect divine inspiration with mathematical knowledge, although skill in computation had always been regarded as a power-giving mystery and 'the key to all obscurities and all that is hidden'. Our authorities for the views of Pythagoras are late and unreliable, but he seems to have tried to replace the religious ritual of the ancient seer with the rational procedure of the philosopher. Pythagoras' method was probably not deduction from axioms, but rather a process for acquiring an intuitive apprehension of mathematical theorems. The function of knowledge thus obtained was neither practical in the ordinary sense, nor was it the satisfaction of curiosity for its own sake, it had a moral or religious function. There can be little doubt that Pythagoras was responsible for the introduction of the religious notion of personal salvation into philosophy, and also for the notion that salvation is to be attained by some kind of rational procedure culminating in metaphysical knowledge (rather than by religious exercises and purifications). For further information, see K.Freeman *Companion to the Pre-Socratic Philosophers* (Oxford, 1947), and F.M. Cornford, *Principium Sapientiae* (Cambridge, 1951).

3. The method of proof from axioms has been practised in mathematics for more than two thousand years, but a precise specification of what constitutes a proof has been accomplished only in the last century. The object of the process of formalization is to eliminate intuition as far as possible, in favour of mechanical manipulation of symbol patterns according to previously specified rules. A *proof* is then defined as a finite sequence of expressions, each member of the sequence being either an axiom or obtained from previous members by a single application of one of the rules. A proof is a proof of the last member of this sequence of expressions. An expression is provable (or derivable) if there is a proof of it. A set of axioms and rules, together with all the expressions which can be

proved from the axioms by means of the rules, is called a formal deductive system.

4. There are two main problems in connexion with a formal deductive system, the problems of consistency and completeness. A system is consistent if no false propositions are provable in it. It is complete if every true proposition (which is expressible in it) is provable. If a system is broad enough, many propositions about the structure of the system itself can be expressed in it. For example, in some system S, we may be able to express the propositions 'S is consistent' and 'S is complete'. There is nothing wrong or paradoxical about this. It was at one time supposed that, since these propositions can be expressed in S, they might also be provable in S (and, of course, true). If this supposition had been correct, appeal to intuition would have been finally expelled from mathematics. It has, however, been shown that 'S is consistent' is provable in S if and only if 'S is inconsistent' is also provable. Thus, such a system must be either inconsistent or incomplete. Recent investigations tend to suggest that a complete formalization of mathematical reasoning can never be accomplished. Thus the metaphysical aim of the deduction of *all* true propositions from a finite number of axioms is almost certainly impossible. For further information on formal systems, see S. C. Kleene, *Introduction to Meta-mathematics* (New York, 1951).

5. If etymology is any guide, knowledge is most often associated with (1) vision (insight, intuition, enlightenment, etc.), (2) skill (know how, cunning), (3) grasp or penetration (apprehend, comprehend, perceive). The visual element in epistemological terminology was ingeniously connected with the skill element by Plato, with his theory of Forms. The result was a theory in which skill in doing something well was seen as an inevitable consequence of a clear vision of what you wanted to do. Hence virtue (the skilful conduct of life and affairs) is identified with knowledge (a clear conception of what to do). Stress on the visual element is associated with a notion of the acquisition of knowledge as a passive reception of something by the mind. This passivity is very prominent in empiricism (for example, Hume says impressions force themselves in upon the understanding, etc.); indeed, the only function left to the mind is that of receiving impressions. Even Berkeley, who does his best to view the mind as an active entity, is fighting against the implications of his terminology. Stress on the grasping or

penetrating analogy of knowledge is associated with a conception of the acquisition of knowledge as an aggressive overcoming of something and its incorporation into the self. The philosophy of Spinoza exhibits this tendency. For example, Spinoza says that a man becomes free in so far as he knows the causes of his actions, and by this he means that a man becomes free in so far as he incorporates the causes of his actions, which is to say in so far as the causes of a man's actions are part of him and not something outside. The ultimate aim of a Spinozistic philosopher is to swallow and digest the universe. But the words for metaphysical knowledge (intuition, contemplation, etc.) have almost always stressed the visual passive aspect.

6. Hume adopts the rationalist account of logical truths. According to this account a logically true statement expresses a relation between ideas, and the occurrence of false beliefs in the field of logic is explained by a supposed vagueness or obscurity in the ideas involved (or in our apprehension of them). Ignorance of logical and mathematical truths may also be explained in this way. For example, there are many propositions about prime numbers whose truth or falsity is still unknown. The rationalist maintains that, if we had a clear and adequate conception of prime numbers (which cannot then be conveyed in the standard definition), the truth of all true propositions about primes, and the falsity of all false ones, would be immediately obvious to us. The aim of the rationalist is to acquire these clear and adequate ideas, so that ultimately *every* true proposition is as obvious as 'one and one is two'. For him, even deductive inference is just a step to the goal of immediate intuition. The notion of philosophical progress as a progress towards clear and adequate ideas is an inheritance from Plato.

Hume sometimes suggests that ideas may be obscure and confused, and it is difficult to see how he could otherwise account for error in the field of logic. But the possibility of confused ideas is entirely contrary to the spirit of his theory, and he should probably have adopted an empiricist account of logical truth. He does not suppose that the aim of philosophy is the acquisition of clear and adequate ideas.

7. ECU 4. 1–2.

8. One way of taking this step is to adopt a *coherence theory* of truth. To put it crudely, this consists in a willingness to reject later observations as invalid or illusory, if they fail to conform

with an extensive body of scientific theory, well grounded on past observations. If such theories run contrary to what a rough realist would call 'the facts', so much the worse for the facts. Scientists sometimes flirt with the coherence theory in their controversies, but among them this is not usually regarded as virtuous conduct. A coherence theory does obviously enable one to deduce the future from the past, at the cost of driving a wedge between appearance and reality.

9. The philosophical notion of causal *power* is derived from the Aristotelian *dynamic*. The etymologies of words like 'power', 'dynamic', 'force', suggest a common root meaning of 'physical strength', and the idea would then be a projection on to the inanimate world of the human feeling of physical endeavour. Hume rejects this derivation, but his own suggestion that the idea of causal power may be traced to the feeling of mental compulsion, is almost certainly false. There has been no investigation of the relation between the philosophical notion of causal power, and primitive orendistic beliefs.

   The word 'cause', like the Greek *aition*, appears to have been imported into philosophy from legal and social contexts.

10. See A. Wolf, *History*, p. 630.

11. TU 3. 6. 1; ECU 4. 9. 'The mind can never possibly find the effect in the supposed cause, by the most accurate scrutiny and examination.'

12. TU 3. 6. 3; ECU 7. 2. 3. 'From the mere repetition of any past impression, even to infinity, there never will arise any new original idea, such as that of necessary connexion.' Nevertheless, Hume finds himself constrained to produce just such a 'new original idea' in order to supply a meaning for the phrase 'necessary connexion'. His real point is that this new idea, and in fact no idea whatever, can do the work that people have wanted necessary connexions to do.

13. TU 3. 6. 10.

14. ECU 4. 2. 10.

15. Hume never *proves* that matters of fact cannot be intuitively known. A proof would demand a thorough investigation of the nature of logical truths, as well as of factual truths, and of the means of knowing them.

   The modern 'problem of induction' arises from the readiness of many philosophers to accept Hume's empiricism, and their reluctance to accept his scepticism. Most of us seem to want to cling to the hope that *something* about the future can be deduced from the past, even if it be very little. The issue has been much confused by the introduction of considerations of probability, and some have tried to save the situation by admitting that all scientific inference is probable inference. But Hume's sceptical attack applies with equal force to probable inference, for if you cannot deduce certainties you cannot deduce probabilities either.

The sceptical truth is that *no* method of investigation can be used to establish its own validity or applicability. This applies to deduction just as much as to induction. Philosophers try to validate induction by means of deduction, only because they mistakenly think the latter is somehow safer, more secure.

16. Descartes' position was a little more sophisticated than is suggested in the text. He does not suppose that we can doubt everything in the ordinary sense of 'doubt', but rather that we can entertain a sort of second level, or intellectual, or *philosophical* doubt, which is different from everyday doubt, and is in fact compatible with everyday certainty. Nowadays it is usual to distinguish philosophical doubts about, for example, the existence of material objects, from everyday doubts, or *real* doubts. There is some similarity between philosophical doubts and neurotic obsessional doubts, which the sufferer cannot help feeling, although he knows very well that they are quite unfounded. The resemblance has been noted by Professor John Wisdom in his book *Philosophy and Psychoanalysis*.

17. ECU 5. 1. 8.
18. TU 3. 2. 15; 3. 14. 1.
19. TU 3. 2. 6.
20. TU 3. 8. 10; ECU 5. 1. 5. 'All inferences from experience, therefore, are the effects of custom, not of reasoning.'
21. TU 3. 14. 35; 3. 14. 31.
22. TU 3. 14. 25.
23. TU 3. 14. 19.
24. TU 4. 1. 5.

CHAPTER 5

1. 'Knowledge is virtue' is much more of a truism in Greek than it is in English. The sort of knowledge intended is that possessed by the trained artisan, i.e. skill, or know how. And just as the *arete* (virtue, excellence) of the shoemaker consists

in his skill at doing what is proper to shoemakers, i.e. making shoes, so the *arete* of man in general consists in his skill at doing whatever is proper to man *qua* man. Thus moral philosophy became the quest of an end, or purpose for man. It seems to have been supposed that this purpose would be revealed in the real definition of man (just as the shoemaker's end or purpose (or job) is exhibited in the definition of 'shoemaker'). The definition of man is 'rational animal', and so his end or purpose is the exercise of reason, and the attainment thereby of contemplative wisdom. This is the 'end for man'.

2. TP 3. 3. 1. Hume's observations on the will are modelled on Locke, *Essay* 21, from whom he quotes, without acknowledgement.

3. TP 3. 3. 2.

4. TP 3. 3. 3.

4. TP 3. 10. Hume naturally identifies the love of truth with simple curiosity, and makes much of our natural satisfaction in exercising our intellectual powers. Curiosity is an appetite like any other. It is not for him, as it was for the metaphysicians, the supreme object of human endeavour and the road to salvation.

6. TM 1. 1. 27.

7. Plato's dialogue *Theaetetus* contains a good collection of such words. Generally speaking, the Greek epistemological vocabulary stresses the notions of visual perception and manual skill. The notion of grasping or penetrating is also present, but this is found more strongly in Latin.

8. These remarks should be reconsidered in connexion with the results of Chapter 7.

9. TM 3. 3.; EPM 5.

10. TM 1. 2; EPM 1.

11. Other sources for Hume's views on religion are: the *Essay on the Natural History of Religion* (NHR), and EHU 10, 11.

In NHR Hume tries to show how religious beliefs in fact originated. The value of such work was naturally limited by the anthropological data available in the eighteenth century. By a religious belief he appears to mean 'belief of invisible, intelligent power'. He observes that such beliefs are not universal, and so cannot 'spring from an original instinct implanted in human nature'. He then tries to show (1) that polytheism, the belief in many gods, everywhere has temporal precedence over monotheism, and (2) that polytheism originates in hope and fear, 'especially the latter', which in turn spring from ignorance concerning the causation of striking natural phenomena. His final attitude to religious beliefs, that is to say his conscious and reasoned attitude, is summed up in the following passage:

> What a noble privilege is it of the human reason to attain know-ledge of the supreme Being; and, from the visible works of nature, be enabled to infer so sublime a principle as its supreme Creator! But turn to the reverse of the medal. Survey most nations and most ages. Examine the religious principles, which have, in fact, pre-vailed in the world. You will scarcely be persuaded, that they are any thing but sick men's dreams.

In EHU 10, Hume argues that no amount of testimony can suffice to prove a miracle. A miracle is an event which trans-gresses the laws of nature; usually, it is supposed, one of the more obvious laws. Hume's argument is that the evidence for a natural law vastly exceeds in quantity and weight any evidence which can be brought in favour of the occurrence of a particular transgression of it. The argument seems sound, but it is not clear that Hume is entitled to use it, in view of his theory of the nature of inductive inference, and of the status of our beliefs in natural laws.

12. For example, the Homeric Zeus did not create the world, nor was he much concerned with the morality of mankind. Rhadamanthus was a judge of the dead, but he was not a creator, nor was he worshipped. Ocean and Tethys were, according to Aristotle, 'the fathers of creation', but were neither moral governors nor objects of worship. Aphrodite was worshipped, the classical view was that she did not create the world, she never concerned herself much with morality. Christianity is a very misleading guide to the aims and content of religions in general.

13. DNR II. 9.

14. One reason for introducing a theory of innate ideas, or rather one motive, is to provide for the idea of God (which meta-physicians admit is not derived from experience). The rationalist argument, exemplified in the work of Descartes, runs roughly as follows: we have the idea of God, this idea cannot be derived from experience, therefore we have ideas not derived from experience. It is then said that the idea of God must come from some source, and that source must contain at least as much as is in the idea (by the principle *ex*

nihilo nihil fit), and the only possible source is God. Therefore, since the idea of God exists, God must exist. Even if the *ex nihilo* principle is true, the validity of its application in this instance is not very obvious.

The empiricist argument ought to be, as it were, the inverse of the above. That is: all ideas are derived from experience, the idea of God, if there were such an idea, would not be derived from experience, therefore we have no idea of God. But neither Locke nor Hume, least of all Berkeley, argues in this way.

15. On the other hand, of course, there is nothing in Hume's theory against the hypothesis that moral conduct is very displeasing to God. It is likely that Hume believed that, if there is a God, he is completely indifferent to human activites. This is the common sceptical opinion.

16. DNR 11.

17. TP 3. 1; EHU 8.

CHAPTER 6

1. TU 1. 7; ECU 2. 9. Hume follows Berkeley's attack on abstract ideas, and refers to Berkeley, PHK 18 (Berkeley's attack really begins at PHK 8).

There are two main theories of abstract ideas: (1) Plato's theory, which involves the notion of perfection, (2) the Epicurean 'composite photograph' theory. For Plato the idea 'man' was a sort of perfect model or prototype, to which actual existing men approached more or less closely. Particular men were said to 'partake' of the idea 'man', or embody it, so to speak, to a greater or lesser degree. Our use of the word 'ideal' to mean 'perfect' presumably derives from this source. For the Epicureans, and many subsequent philosophers, the idea 'man' was formed in the mind by superposition of many impressions, something like those composite photographs anthropologists used to take in order to get a picture of a standard European, Australian, etc. But the eighteenth-century attacks on abstract ideas are not directed specifically against either of these theories. Some other interest seems to be involved. For Berkeley, at any rate, the theory of abstract ideas seems to have represented all the philosophical dust that has ever been raised.

2. These points were established in Chapter 3.

3. Hume's attitude to common sense was to some extent shared by the Sceptics of antiquity; see Chapter 7.

4. Reid (1710–96) was the founder of the Scottish common-sense school. His chief works are *Inquiry into the Human Mind on the principles of Common Sense* (1764), and *Essays on the Intellectual Powers of Man*. Reid argued that (1) our common-sense beliefs about the external world are true, (2) Hume's conclusions are incompatible with those beliefs, therefore (3) Hume's conclusions are false, (4) Hume's conclusions are impeccably deduced from his premises (i.e. the sensualist theory of ideas), therefore (5) Hume's premises are false. Hume would have accepted only (2) and (4); in fact, (4) is also very doubtful.

5. TU 4. 2. 38.

6. TU 4. 2. 36; 43. There are three different theories about the relation between a perception and a material object, which makes that perception a perception *of* that object:

   (1) The perception is identical with the object;
   (2) The perception is caused by, or represents the object;
   (3) The perception is a member of a class of perceptions which constitute the object.

   The second theory is adopted by Locke, Essay 2. 8, and is strongly attacked by Hume. The first theory, which Hume attributes to the 'vulgar', has been attacked by several writers on the following grounds: (a) perceptions cannot change and material objects can, (b) material objects can have unseen parts (back, inside, etc.) and perceptions cannot, (c) perceptions are always exactly as they appear, and material objects are not. If any one or more of these three propositions is accepted (and they all seem to be accepted by Hume) as definitive of the entities in question, it is *logically impossible* for perceptions to be identical with material objects, and therefore exceptionally difficult to understand how the vulgar could confuse them (especially on Hume's theory that what is logically impossible is unimaginable). Modern writers have tended to fall back on some form of (3). Professor H. H. Price, in his monograph *Hume's theory of the External World* (p. 98), tries to attribute (3) to Hume and the vulgar, but Hume at least seems to me to be so definite on this point that it is impossible to ascribe (3) to him.

7. TU 4. 2. 50.

8. The tower which appears small and round in the distance and large and square close to has been a stock philosophical example ever since the time of Lucretius (98–54 B.C.).
9. TU 4. 2. 12.
10. See Chapter 4. If Hume had completed his theory of the external world the obvious step would have been to reject the three propositions of note 6, and admit that perceptions can change, etc. He could still have held that they do not in fact do so. But it is not altogether clear that he must have taken this step. It is perhaps one thing to confuse two logically distinct kinds of object, and another to suppose the existence of something that logically cannot exist.
11. TU 4. 2. 40.
12. TU 4. 2. 18; 19.
13. TU 4. 2. 20–4. Professor Price (note 6) discusses this matter at length, but his treatment is complicated by his identification of Hume's impressions with his own 'sensibilia'. Professor Price's sensibilia are capable of existing unperceived, but they have (presumably by definition) only a momentary existence. The latter is not the case with Hume's impressions.
14. TU 4. 2. 25–34.
15. TU 4. 2. 45. What these 'experiments' prove is that, assuming suitable definitions of 'perception' and 'material object', perceptions cannot be identical with material objects. This is the conclusion usually drawn in modern times.
16. But he nearly always writes as if he had finally proved that perceptions had no continued existence.
17. Hume's account of the external world is technically incomplete for the reasons given in note 6. A complete and satisfactory account has not yet been given along these lines. For more recent attempts the reader should consult H. H. Price (as in note 6), A. J. Ayer Foundations of Empirical Knowledge, etc.
18. TU 4. 6. 2.
19. TU 4. 6. 4. He continues with a more picturesque description:

The mind is a kind of theatre, where several perceptions successively make their appearance; pass, repass, glide away, and mingle in an infinite variety of postures and situations. There is properly no simplicity in it at one time, nor identity in different; whatever natural propensions we may have to imagine that simplicity and identity. The comparison of the theatre must not mislead us. They are the successive perceptions only, that constitute the mind; nor have we the most distant notion of the place, where

173

these scenes are represented, or of the materials of which they are composed.

20. That is to say, two particles are in the same cloud if either (*a*) they are less than the maximum permissible distance from one another, or (*b*) there is a finite chain of particles, each of which is less than the maximum permissible distance from its neighbours, and the particles in question are in such a chain.
21. TU 4. 6. 16–19.
22. TU 4. 6. 6–14.
23. TU 4. 6. 18; 19.
24. TU Appendix.
25. The curious link between shape and function in some cases (we readily say that something is 'functionally designed', and such objects have a certain aesthetic appeal) is one possible psychological source for the Platonic theory of Forms.
26. This feature of primitive thought has been much commented on by anthropologists (e.g. J.G.Frazer, *The Golden Bough*). In savage communities there is no such thing as natural or accidental (i.e. uncaused) death. The few remaining unpredictable phenomena, e.g. the weather, are still the subject of prayer in our churches.
27. Berkeley regarded material objects as nothing but bundles of sensible qualities (PHK I): 'a certain colour, taste, smell, figure, and consistence having been observed to go together, are accounted one distinct thing, signified by the name *apple*.' But Berkeley, like Locke before him, identifies perceptions with qualities.
28. There may, of course, be some modified form of empiricism which escapes this conclusion.

CHAPTER 7

1. The works of Sextus Empiricus, who lived about A.D. 200, are available in the Loeb Classical Library, together with an English translation by Rev.R.G.Bury. The only work quoted in these notes is the *Outlines of Pyrrhonism*.

    According to Mossner, *Life*, p. 128, the resemblance between certain of Hume's arguments and those of Sextus were noted by a reviewer of the first edition of the *Treatise* in *Bibliotheque Raisonnée* for April–June 1740. I have not been able to verify the reference; according to Mossner the reviewer mentions Sextus, OP 3. 3, which does not seem very appropriate.

It is not known if Hume had read Sextus at the time of composition of the *Treatise*. His knowledge of Greek was inadequate for the purpose, but the edition of J.A.Fabricius (Leipzig, 1718) included the Latin version of H.Stephens, which Hume was probably capable of reading. The only reference to Sextus in Hume's philosophical writings occurs at *Essay on the Natural History of Religion*, 4 (1757). There can be no question of plagiarism. Hume's analysis is far more subtle and thorough than anything attempted by Sextus.

2. Sextus, OP 1. 3.
3. Sextus, OP 1. 12; 1. 13.
4. Sextus, OP 1. 19.
5. ECU 5. 8; 1. 12; TU Introduction 8.
6. Sextus, OP 2. 97.
7. Sextus, OP 2. 100; TU 3. 14. 31.
8. Hume himself is at some pains to distinguish his kind of scepticism from what he calls 'Pyrrhonism', and this demands some explanation. The term 'Pyrrhonism' is derived from the name of Pyrrho of Elis, who flourished about 300 B.C. The exact nature of Pyrrho's teachings is unknown, but we may assume that Sextus is a fair guide. Thus, in its original connotation Pyrrhonism is very similar to the scepticism taught by Hume. The term became debased in meaning by a confusion of Scepticism with the opinions and methods of the later Sophists. The confusion was facilitated by the fact, amongst others, that many of the dialectical weapons employed by the Sceptics were forged by the Sophists. But the difference in their aims is decisive. The Sceptics aimed at peace of mind and the undogmatic acceptance of common sense. The Sophist's aim was simply to confuse and refute his opponent by whatever means lay to hand. In the Sophistic schools philosophy degenerated into an unedifying verbal struggle, in which a species of linguistic lifemanship was of greater value than any real philosophical ability.
9. Sextus, OP 1. 8; 12; 202.
10. T Introduction 9.
11. For example, there are two ways in which we can be said to know a person. (1) We know Mr X in the sense of knowing him by sight, we can recognize him when we meet him, we can pick him out at identification parades. (2) We know Mr X

in the sense of knowing his character, habits, background, and business. When we know someone in this second sense, we know, so to speak, his 'place', we know how to behave towards him and what to expect from him. So also with animals, it is one thing to be able to recognize them, another to know their habits and manner of life, and the way they fit into the ecological scheme. And so, it has been thought, with things in general. The 'real nature' of a thing is what determines its place or status, in this quasi-social sense, in the natural world. Clearly the 'real nature' of a thing is not revealed by simple inspection, because we can learn to recognize a thing without knowing thereby its status. The concept of 'real natures' has a fundamental role in rationalist philosophy, and is what is conveyed in a real definition, or by 'clear and adequate ideas'. The result of the peculiar methods of rationalist enquiry (usually based on Plato's dialectic) is supposed to be an intuitive insight into 'real natures'.

12. In the Epicureans and Sceptics it is fear of death, or more accurately of 'what comes after death', and possibly fear of the imagined activities of supernatural beings, that provides the motive for philosophical activity. Thus Epicurus (Bailey, 81) says:

> The principle disturbance in the minds of men arises because they think that these celestial bodies are blessed and immortal, and yet have wills and actions and motives inconsistent with these attributes; and because they are always expecting some everlasting misery, such as is depicted in legends, or even fear the loss of feeling in death as though it would concern themselves; and, again, because they are brought to this pass not by reasoned opinion, but rather by some irrational presentiment etc.

The attainment of *ataraxy*, Epicurus tells us, is the aim of his philosophy, and it is to be gained by removing these irrational fears. Professor F.M.Cornford seems to have been the first to stress this important aspect of Epicureanism.

Hume was never able to conceive of life after death in any but gloomy and terrifying terms, and he universalizes his personal feeling 'terror is the primary principle of religion' (DNR 12). Accounts of his death show that he did in fact attain the *ataraxy* which is the real aim of philosophical scepticism.

It may be doubted that terror is the primary principle of religion, but there is an obvious reason why it should become the strongest feature of an ascetic and ethical religion, such as Christianity. Since mundane pleasures are essentially evil, the nature of our heavenly reward cannot be clearly expressed in terms of anything with which the ordinary person is familiar, and so cannot exercise a strong persuasive influence on the mind. There is no such bar to an impressive delineation of the terrors of Hell.

13. The dialogues of Cicero contain an interesting account of these philosophical systems.

14. Sextus, OP I. 27.

15. There is some difficulty, in these irreligious times, in attaining an imaginative grasp of the power of religious fear. A convincing description of it occurs in James Joyce's novel *Portrait of the Artist as a Young Man.*

16. We know little about Hume's early religious attitudes; the religion of his childhood was Calvinism. His first philosophical writings appear to have been attempts to deal with some kind of religious conflict. In a letter written in middle life he says (Mossner, *Life*, p.64):

> 'Tis not long since that I burned an old Manuscript Book, wrote before I was twenty; which contained, Page after Page, the gradual Progress of my Thoughts on that head. It began with an anxious search after Arguments, to confirm the common Opinion; doubts stole in, dissipated, returned, were again dissipated, returned again; and it was a perpetual struggle of a restless imagination against Inclination, perhaps against Reason.

Whatever may have been Hume's motives in burning this book, the student of his thought can but regret the occurrence. It must have contained something much more personal and enlightening than the abstract arguments for religious scepticism suggested by Professor Mossner. Reasoned argument may sometimes be the occasion of religious conversion, but it is never the cause.

The nature of Hume's religious feelings, as distinct from his consciously held views, is suggested by a letter of James Caulfield (Lord Charlemont) describing the philosopher's illness in Turin in 1748. 'In the Paroxysms of his Disorder he often talked, with much seeming Perturbation, of the Devil, of Hell, and of Damnation.' Caulfield continues: 'we all agreed in laughing at the Philosopher's fears and desparation.' George Norvell alleged that Hume at this time 'received extreme unction'. Mossner (*Life*, p.218) doubts the truth of this on general grounds, but suggests that Hume's friends may have foisted some such mummery on him by way of a practical joke, when he was, or believed himself to be, at the point of death.

17. ECU 12. 3. 11; TU 4. 7. 8.
18. TU 4. 7. 9.
19. Sextus, OP I. 29.
20. Locke, EHU Epistle 4; 5.
21. Locke, EHU I. I. 6.
22. Locke, EHU 4. 3. 29; 4. 12. 10.
23. Locke, EHU 4. 12. 11.
24. Locke, EHU 4. 10.
25. Berkeley, PHK Preface.
26. Berkeley, PHK Introduction 3.
27. Berkeley, PHK Introduction 6.
28. Berkeley, PHK 2; 27.
29. Berkeley, PHK 101.
30. Berkeley, PHK 109; 108 (edition of 1710). Berkeley has the optimistic notion that evil is unreal, and that apparent evils are necessary parts of God's great good plan. Thus:

We shall be forced to acknowledge that those particular things, which considered in themselves appear to be *evil*, have the nature of *good*, when considered as *linked with the whole system of beings* (PHK 153).

31. Berkeley, PHK 155; 156.

INDEX

INDEX

Human nature, blindness of, 23
  improvement of, 87
  investigation of, 20
  metaphysical view of, 21

Ideas, confusion of, 30
  copies of impressions, 34
  faint images, 33
  relations of, 65
  simple and complex, 34
Identity, numerical and qualitative, 122
  personal, 128
Imagination, coextensive with possible experience, 27
  ideas of, 38
  limits of, 24
Impressions, force and liveliness of, 33, 37
  priority of simple, 35, 37
  of reflexion, 34
  simple, 34
Inference, deductive, 60
  causal, 73
  probable, 80–5
Intuition, 60

Knowledge, conditions of, 79–80
  contrasted with natural beliefs, 65
  no direct influence on conduct, 89
  divine, 58
  intuitive, 60
  ordinary and metaphysical, 21
  scientific, 57
  theory of, 56, 63
  and virtue, 87

Liberty, an illusion, 22

Man, science of, 19
Material objects, and perceptions, 113–20

Mathematics, a model of knowledge, 59
Meaning, and ideas, 30, 113
  and feigning, 31–2
Memory, ideas of, 38
Metaphysics, aims of, 21
  rejection of, 150
  and religion, 152
  and superstition, 151
Mind, as a bundle of perceptions, 47, 128
  considered as a medium, 47
  inadequacy of Hume's account, 131–2
  not a perception, 127
  three theories of, 126
Moral, approval, 103
  codes, 96
  conduct, its function, 110
  dread and the supernatural, 147
  improvement, 87
  judgement a matter of taste, 104
  knowledge, 88, 104
  persuasion, 87–8
  virtue, 21
Motive, and belief, 90
  and desire, 91

Nature, uniformity of, 64
  real, 146
Necessity, 74

Occult, futility of belief in the, 69, 70, 136
  matters, 141
  objects, 29, 30
  powers, 68
Ontological proof for the existence of God, 39
Ought, not derivable from 'is', 94

Passions, as the source of evil, 21, 86
  reason their slave, 22